365 DAYS of PLAY

Sara Miller McCune founded SAGE Publishing in 1965 to support the dissemination of usable knowledge and educate a global community. SAGE publishes more than 1000 journals and over 800 new books each year, spanning a wide range of subject areas. Our growing selection of library products includes archives, data, case studies and video. SAGE remains majority owned by our founder and after her lifetime will become owned by a charitable trust that secures the company's continued independence.

Los Angeles | London | New Delhi | Singapore | Washington DC | Melbourne

365 DAYS of PLAY

ALISTAIR BRYCE-CLEGG

CORWIN

A SAGE company
2455 Teller Road
Thousand Oaks, California 91320
(0800)233-9936
www.corwin.com

SAGE Publications Ltd
1 Oliver's Yard
55 City Road
London EC1Y 1SP

SAGE Publications India Pvt Ltd
B 1/I 1 Mohan Cooperative Industrial Area
Mathura Road
New Delhi 110 044

SAGE Publications Asia-Pacific Pte Ltd
3 Church Street
#10-04 Samsung Hub
Singapore 049483

Editor: Amy Thornton
Senior project editor: Chris Marke
Marketing Manager: Lorna Patkai
Design: Wendy Scott
Typeset by: C&M Digitals (P) Ltd, Chennai, India

Library of Congress Control Number: 2019954067

British Library Cataloguing in Publication Data

A catalogue record for this book is available from
the British Library

ISBN 978-1-5264-6447-7
ISBN 978-1-5264-6448-4 (pbk)

ABOUT ME...
Alistair Bryce-Clegg

After teaching in a number of schools in Manchester and Trafford I became Head teacher of a three-form entry Infant school and Early Years Unit in Cheshire where I spent 10 happy years.

Towards the end of this time I established a consultancy career specialising in the education of children in the Early Years and left headship in 2009 to set up ABC Does...

Most of my time is spent working with practitioners in individual settings or as part of larger projects with various Local Authorities. I also run conferences and deliver keynotes both nationally and internationally.

I've written for various magazines and other publications and working with Bloomsbury have published over 20 books.

I have an MA in teaching and am now studying for my Doctorate in Early Years.

I'm passionate about inspiring children to reach their potential and equipping practitioners with the skills and enthusiasm to achieve this.

ABOUT THIS BOOK

The idea for the book *365 Days of Play* came about because I literally spend 365 days a year thinking and talking about the importance (and joy) of play!

For all humans, children and adults, what we play is what we know and what we experience. Sometimes our play will replicate real life, sometimes fantasy and often a mixture of both. Children can imagine possibilities, think of possible outcomes to a specific scenario and then test their thoughts.

Play is crucial to our social development. It helps us to become familiar with our own preferences and feelings as well as learn to recognise the emotional state of others. A lack of play opportunities means that we do not get enough time to observe, practise and rehearse the subtleties of social signaling which make us effective and appropriate communicators.

Play is one of the only places where children are actively able to mix the realms of fantasy and reality either as a solo experience or alongside others. It is the element of play that keeps them safe. It allows them to practise, imagine and rehearse problems and possibilities before they happen.

Lots of opportunities to do this will equip children not with the solutions to every eventuality they will come up against, but the strategies for problem solving and a wealth of experience to draw upon.

Playing with other children not only reinforces social interactions but gives the children involved the opportunity to learn about the thoughts, reactions and strategies of others, which will in turn enhance their own!

Research has shown that play stimulates the brain nerve growth in the part of the brain where emotions and decisions are processed. Basically, play is essential for sorting out how the world makes you and others feel and making decisions about what you need to do next.

I wanted *365 Days of Play* to be a source of inspiration for people to dip in and out of. The book includes other people's thoughts and words about the importance of play as well as my own. I also wanted to include a (very) brief history of some of the people who have influenced how we view the role of play in education today.

It is a book that you can sit down and read as a whole, pick up when you need a bit of inspiration or read a page a day for a year! However people choose to use it, the primary aim of the book is to reinforce the need for play, the essential and positive impact of play and the fact that it is a fundamental right of children (and adults) to play as often and for as long as possible!

It only takes the tiny spark

... of idea to start the fire of play.

THEORISTS AND PHILOSOPHERS

WHAT WE THINK, AND THE INFORMATION THAT WE KNOW ABOUT THE IMPORTANCE OF PLAY AND ITS IMPACT ON CHILDREN'S LEARNING HAS BEEN GATHERED OVER MANY YEARS BY PEOPLE WHO HAVE MADE IT THEIR LIFE'S WORK TO OBSERVE COUNTLESS CHILDREN AT PLAY AND TO STUDY THE IMPACT OF THAT PLAY ON THEIR DEVELOPMENT.

WHILST ADVANCES IN SCIENCE HAVE DISPROVED SOME OF THE IDEAS OF THE EARLY THEORISTS, MANY UNDERPIN OUR PHILOSOPHY OF PLAY TODAY. THROUGHOUT THIS BOOK, YOU WILL COME ACROSS SOME (BUT BY NO MEANS ALL) OF THE MOST INFLUENTIAL THINKERS AND PRACTITIONERS WHO HAVE SHAPED OUR THINKING AND PRACTICE.

THEY ARE MY PLAY HEROES!

PLAY IS THE ONLY WAY THE HIGHEST INTELLIGENCE OF HUMANKIND CAN UNFOLD.

– JOSEPH CHILTON PEARCE

NATURE AND EARLY MATHEMATICS SKILLS

EXPERIENCING OUTDOOR PLAY CAN HELP CHILDREN TO DISCOVER AND HONE MANY IMPORTANT SKILLS SUCH AS MATHEMATICS.

- The stones on a path
- The veins of a leaf
- The stripes on a bee

All linked to early mathematics skills.

Play, while it cannot
change the external realities
of children's lives, can be a vehicle
for children to explore and enjoy their
differences and similarities and to create,
even for a brief time, a more just
world where everyone is an equal
and valued participant.

PATRICIA G. RAMSEY

In the HANDBOOK OF CHILD PSYCHOLOGY, Kenneth Rubin characterised play as behaviour that is:

Intrinsically MOTIVATED

FOCUSED on MEANS rather than ends

Distinct from exploratory behaviour

Non literal (involves pretence)

FREE from EXTERNALLY IMPOSED RULES

ACTIVELY (not just passively) engaged in by the players

THE ANCIENT GREEKS

It seems that play and education has been a hot topic of discussion for centuries. The subject made an appearance in the work of the ancient Greek philosophers Plato and Aristotle as far back as 348BC. Although a supporter of play as a means of learning, Plato was very much in favour of children being given the opportunity to 'play' at a profession they would later take on. If children were to become builders then Plato suggested they should be given opportunities to play at building. Plato recognised the fundamental truth that children were more likely to engage with learning, if that learning was linked to play.

Plato also wrote about natural methods of play that children discovered for themselves between the ages of 3 and 6 years old. Whilst he fully supported this type of play until you were 6, he then felt that children's play should be more controlled and guided by adults. Plato's main reasoning for this was that children in unregulated play would often change the rules of the game or even the game itself. Plato worried that if they were allowed to carry on then when they were adults they might attempt to change the rules and laws and upset the status quo.

WHAT IS PLAY?

Play Therapy UK define play as

'A physical or mental leisure activity that is undertaken purely for enjoyment or amusement and has no other objective'.

MARIA MONTESSORI SAID...

Never help a child with a task at which he feels he can succeed.

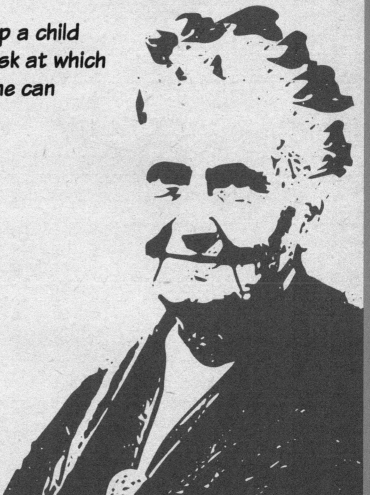

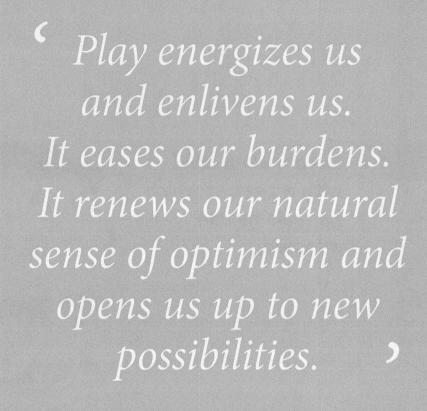

'Play energizes us and enlivens us. It eases our burdens. It renews our natural sense of optimism and opens us up to new possibilities.'

▷ ▷ ▷ Stuart Brown, MD

EARLY PHYSICAL DEVELOPMENT

In her book What Comes Before Phonics?, Sally Neaum discusses the importance of early physical development:

In the first few years of life, children's physical development is prodigious. At birth, neonates have a series of primary reflexes that enable them to root, suckle, grasp, startle (Moro reflex), step and turn (Tonic neck reflex). Motor development then occurs through skeletal and neuro-muscular maturation combined with physical interaction with the environment. This develops children's strength, control and dexterity, and they move from early uncoordinated activity to coordinated motor behaviour (Goddard-Blyth, 2011).

For this to happen, children need opportunities in their early play for a wide range of physical activity. They need appropriate experiences and the time and space to repeatedly practice, develop and refine their physical skills to become increasingly physically competent.

LEAVE ROOM FOR IMAGINATION TO FLOURISH

OPEN ENDED NATURAL MATERIALS STIMULATE CHILDREN'S IMAGINATION

I like playing at the games table because it makes me feel calm. You have to take turns when you are playing games.

NIAMH, AGE 5

LIFE MUST
BE LIVED
AS PLAY

SAINT AUGUSTINE OF HIPPO

Saint Augustine of Hippo (AD 354–430) was not so positive in his account of play and the impact it had on his life. In his catchily entitled writing 'Confessions' he talks about how he had neglected his school work because of his desire to play. The play didn't work out well for him, as he was beaten for doing it! Rather than lament these beatings, he wishes that he had listened to his parents and teachers and worked more and played less. This idea of play being something that distracts you from, rather than prepares you for, adult life is a common theme in early Christian writing. The point that Augustine seems to be missing is that his motivation was to play and it is that motivation that drives the desire to learn.

LANGUAGE

SKILL

THROUGH PLAY CHILDREN CAN . . . .

EXTEND THEIR RANGE OF
VOCABULARY AS WELL
AS MECHANISMS FOR USING
AND EXPRESSING LANGUAGE.

CHILD DEVELOPMENT 0-2 YEARS

Children will use their immediate and direct experience to prompt what they re-enact in their play.

RISK

Through RISKY PLAY children get to see a direct correlation between cause and effect. In any activity that involves an element of speed or physical interaction there is a likelihood that someone might experience a bump here and there. How children's reactions directly affect the physical and emotional well-being of others is a crucial life lesson.

INTERACTIVE DIALOGUE

Through their play, children can talk to others who respond appropriately. They learn the art of conversation, when to speak and the importance of listening.

INTRINSIC AND EXTRINSIC MOTIVATION

In her text *Exploring Play for Early Childhood Studies*, Mandy Andrews discusses intrinsic and extrinsic motivation for play:

'We are told that play can be 'spontaneous and unpredictable'. Children can be motivated to play 'intrinsically' or 'extrinsically':

Intrinsic Motivation is when the prompt or desire to do something comes from inside a person. The individual child wants to take part in the play activity, or feels the need to explore their own abilities or emotions without being prompted by someone else to do so. A child is intrinsically motivated to play when they choose how and when to play, and what they are going to play with. The impulse to play comes from the child and they seek opportunities to pursue their own interests.

Extrinsic Motivation is the motivation, or the pressure to do something, that comes from outside a person. Under extrinsic motivation a child is encouraged by another person, perhaps their teacher or play worker, to take part in a planned activity. They may still enjoy the activity, and may approach the activity 'playfully' and with enthusiasm.'

I like writing stories because it makes me feel happy. I like writing about my family.

UTKARSH, AGE 5

TRANSFORMING OBJECTS

In play, children use their imagination to turn one object into another. The more ambiguous the object, the easier the process. So a box can be

A BOAT

A HOUSE

A MICROWAVE

A SHOE . . .

PLAYING OUTDOORS IS GOOD FOR MENTAL HEALTH

RESEARCH SHOWS THAT PLAYING OUTDOORS IS GOOD FOR MENTAL HEALTH. TIME SPENT OUTSIDE PHYSIOLOGICALLY REDUCES ANXIETY. GIVING CHILDREN THE OPPORTUNITY TO PLAY OUTSIDE CAN HAVE A REALLY POSITIVE IMPACT ON THEIR ENGAGEMENT AND INTERACTIONS WHEN THEY ARE INSIDE.

ALL OF THE DESCRIPTIONS OF HUMAN PLAY CAN BE REDUCED DOWN TO 5 MAIN ELEMENTS

PLAY IS...

- SELF-CHOSEN AND SELF-DIRECTED
- INTRINSICALLY MOTIVATED WHERE THE MEANS ARE MORE VALUED THAN THE ENDS
- IMAGINATIVE
- GUIDED BY MENTAL RULES, BUT THE RULES LEAVE ROOM FOR CREATIVITY
- CONDUCTED IN AN ALERT, ACTIVE, BUT RELATIVELY NON-STRESSED FRAME OF MIND

{PETER GRAY, 2013}

FOR MORE ON THE 5 ELEMENTS OF PLAY, GO TO FEBRUARY 22

PLAY IS TRAINING FOR THE UNEXPECTED.

- MARC BEKOFF

JOHN LOCKE (1632–1704)

Whilst there were lots of negative attitudes to play as frivolous or time wasting, especially within religious communities, there was one philosopher in the 1600s who was taking a different view. Locke felt that children learned best when learning was made into 'a recreation' (play). Children would then enjoy it and want to do it more. He observed how children who had been put under great pressure to learn had gone on to hate learning for the rest of their lives.

John Locke was from a group of thinkers that became known as 'the empiricists'. Empiricists believed that children's learning was made up of the experiences and influences that they came into contact with throughout their lives. To best know how to understand and support children with their future learning, teachers should observe children's behaviours and then structure learning and experiences to support them. Locke realised the importance of a child's experience in shaping how they became an adult. Many of Locke's thoughts and theories underpin our approach to Early Years education today.

WHEN LIFE THROWS YOU A RAINY DAY, PLAY IN THE PUDDLES.

– POOH BEAR

I like playing in the box area. I like making food. I feel happy.

ALYSSA, AGE 5

WHEN YOU'RE FREE, YOU CAN PLAY AND WHEN YOU'RE PLAYING YOU BECOME FREE.

- HEIDI KADUSON

TESTING LIMITS

SUCCESSFUL PLAY SPACES OFFER CHILDREN CHALLENGE AND ACTIVITIES THAT TEST THE LIMITS OF THEIR CAPABILITIES, INCLUDING ROUGH AND TUMBLE, SPORTS AND GAMES, AND OPPORTUNITIES TO CLIMB.

WE DON'T SO MUCH PLAY TO LEARN, BUT WE DO LEARN SO MUCH THROUGH PLAY...

Play underpins learning in all aspects of children's development. As soon as we are able, we are exploring all kinds of intellectual, creative and social skills through our play. Our play is usually spontaneous and self-initiated. We use it to explore and discover the physical world around us and the creatures that inhabit it. Effective play spaces support opportunities for learning through this playful exploration and individual interpretation. They also provide safe but challenging opportunities to support and extend learning and development.

FEBRUARY

SOMETIMES YOU HAVE TO DROP THE RAKE AND PLAY IN THE LEAVES.

- DOUGLAS V'SOSKE

IT IS IMPORTANT TO TAKE TIME TO WATCH, REFLECT AND INTERPRET WHAT YOU SEE WHEN CHILDREN ARE PLAYING. WATCHING IS AS IMPORTANT AS TEACHING BECAUSE WHAT YOU SEE WILL INFORM WHAT YOU TEACH.

PRACTITIONER NOTE

Don't over enhance play provision. No child ever stopped their game of Super Hero baddies and said...

'I know we are having a brilliant game of chasing but let's just stop here for a moment and access this lovely number line and use it in our play!'

It just doesn't happen!

ALMOST ALL CREATIVITY INVOLVES PURPOSEFUL PLAY.

– ABRAHAM MASLOW

JEAN-JACQUES ROUSSEAU
(1712–1778)

Rousseau challenged much of the thinking that was around when he was writing. He was a huge advocate for children learning through play. He agreed with a great deal of what John Locke had said but took it even further. Rousseau proposed a radical (for the time) theory that children went through stages of development and that their education should mirror these stages. From birth to 12 years old children were influenced by impulses and emotions that they should be encouraged to explore. From 12 to 16 years old he believed that children developed the ability to reason and that became their predominant driving force.

He also felt that all of the games that children played had the potential for learning and that what children learned through play was infinitely more valuable than what they learned in the classroom. Rousseau made strong links between children's happiness and their learning. He was an early proponent of the concept of well-being being central to how children learn and progress. He also advocated the importance of children making strong bonds with their parents in the early stages of life and was an advocate of mothers to breast feed to create this bond when lots of children of the age would have been passed on to a wet nurse for feeding. In 1762 Rousseau recorded his thinking in his book *Emile*.

I like building castles on the lightbox. It makes me feel good because I love castles.

FAREYHA, AGE 5

CHILD DEVELOPMENT

IN THEIR 2ND YEAR...

CHILDREN BEGIN TO
ENGAGE IN SYMBOLIC PLAY.

A doll will represent a baby,
and blocks will become
a garage or a house.

IF YOU WANT TO BE CREATIVE, STAY IN PART A CHILD, WITH THE CREATIVITY AND INVENTION THAT CHARACTERIZES CHILDREN BEFORE THEY ARE DEFORMED BY ADULT SOCIETY.

- JEAN PIAGET

THE CHILD'S NEEDS
SUSAN ISAACS, 1937

Warm Human Relationships

Real & Active Experience

Security

Opportunity for Self-Assertion & Independence

PLAY with other children

WHOEVER
WANTS TO
UNDERSTAND
MUCH MUST
PLAY MUCH.
— GOTTFRIED BENN

PLAYING OUTSIDE HELPS CHILDREN TO COMMUNICATE . . .

BOTH VERBALLY AND NON-VERBALLY. THEY NEED TO DISCUSS AND CLARIFY THE RULES IN THEIR INVENTED GAMES.

ASK FOR HELP WITH BUILDING OR CLIMBING. SHARE IDEAS FOR STORY TELLING AND FANTASY PLAY. THEY WILL NEED TO ASK QUESTIONS AND SHOW THEY UNDERSTAND THE ANSWERS WHILST ALSO MAKING THEMSELVES UNDERSTOOD.

'Stand aside for a while and leave room for learning, observe carefully what children do, and then, if you have understood well, perhaps teaching will be different from before.'

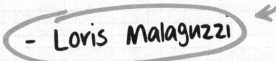

- Loris Malaguzzi

100 TRILLION SYNAPSES

BETWEEN AGES 1 AND 2 YEARS OLD, A TODDLER'S CEREBRAL CORTEX ADDS MORE THAN 2 MILLION NEW SYNAPSES (CONNECTIONS BETWEEN BRAIN CELLS) EVERY SECOND.

BY AGE 2, THEY HAVE MORE THAN 100 TRILLION SYNAPSES, THE MOST THEY'LL EVER HAVE IN THEIR LIFE. STIMULATING THE BRAIN AND OFFERING CHILDREN NEW AND CHALLENGING EXPERIENCES SUPPORTS THIS PROCESS. ONE OF THE BEST WAYS TO SUPPORT THAT DEVELOPMENT IS TO LET CHILDREN PLAY.

CREATIVE PEOPLE ARE CURIOUS, FLEXIBLE, PERSISTENT AND INDEPENDENT WITH A TREMENDOUS SPIRIT OF ADVENTURE AND LOVE OF PLAY.

- HENRI MATISSE

THE FREEDOM OF SPACE

Helen Bilton, author of 'Playing Outside' describes one of the benefits of outdoor play.

OUTSIDE is a natural environment for children. There is a freedom associated with the space which cannot be replicated inside. If children feel at home in a particular space it seems natural to teach them in that area; education should not be a chore but an enjoyable worthwhile occupation. Children playing and learning in an outdoor environment appear more active, absorbed, motivated and purposeful, and develop a more positive attitude to learning.

For more from Helen Bilton
see 26th of April and the 12th of July.

ROLE TAKING
UNDER DIRECTION
(COOPERATION)

SKILL

THROUGH PLAY CHILDREN CAN . . .

LEARN TO COOPERATE
BUT ARE HAPPY TO BE
DIRECTED BY ANOTHER CHILD
OR ADULT WHO IS LEADING
THE SCENARIO.

A LITTLE NONSENSE NOW AND THEN IS CHERISHED BY THE WISEST MEN.

– ROALD DAHL

JOHANN PESTALOZZI (1746–1827)

The work of Rousseau seriously influenced the thinking of Johann Pestalozzi who went on to earn himself the, not insignificant, title of 'The Father of Modern Education'. Pestalozzi had an interesting journey to becoming an education reformer, working as a clergyman, a politician and a farmer, before settling on education. It was taking on all of those roles that let him experience the truth of the society he lived in, including the number of children living in extreme poverty.

Initially Pestalozzi created a school for peasant children where his idea was that the children would fund their own education by selling produce that they would create. The plan failed, causing Pestalozzi to fundamentally rethink his approach.

Pestalozzi eventually settled on a philosophy of education that emphasised the development of the whole child, which encompasses all aspects including the 'head, heart and hands'. He believed that children should be led by their interests and learn from the environment that surrounds them.

He was also an advocate of children being able to think and reason answers for themselves rather than being told or instructed by the teacher. Even though he lived hundreds of years ago, there are many elements of Pestalozzi's thinking that run through the guidance for teaching children in the Early Years today. You need go no further than The Characteristics of Effective Learning to hear the echoes of his voice.

YOU LEARN BETTER WHEN YOU ARE HAVING FUN

WHEN YOU'RE HAVING FUN, YOU BOOST YOUR POSITIVE EMOTIONS WHICH ACTIVATE THE LEARNING CENTRES IN YOUR BRAIN. THAT MEANS YOU ARE CONNECTING WITH MORE OF THE BRAIN POWER YOU HAVE AND HENCE YOU'LL BE MORE ALERT IN NOTICING NEW THINGS AND LEARNING THROUGH THEM. WHEN YOU'RE HAVING FUN, YOU'RE ALSO MUCH MORE CREATIVE AND INNOVATIVE WHICH MEANS YOU'LL BE ABLE TO ENGAGE WITH WHATEVER YOU'RE LEARNING THROUGH COMING UP WITH NEW IDEAS AS WELL AS CHALLENGING THINGS.

ALISTAIR BRYCE-CLEGG

Here We Go Round the Mulberry Bush

Here we go round the mulberry bush
The mulberry bush, the mulberry bush
Here we go round the mulberry bush
So early in the morning

This is the way we wash our clothes
Wash our clothes, wash our clothes
This is the way we wash our clothes
So early Monday morning

This is the way we iron our clothes
Iron our clothes, iron our clothes
This is the way we iron our clothes
So early Tuesday morning

This is the way we mend our clothes
Mend our clothes, mend our clothes
This is the way we mend our clothes
So early Wednesday morning

This is the way we sweep the floor
Sweep the floor, sweep the floor
This is the way we sweep the floor
So early Thursday morning

This is the way we scrub the floor
Scrub the floor, scrub the floor
This is the way we scrub the floor
So early Friday morning

This is the way we bake our bread
Bake our bread, bake our bread
This is the way we bake our bread
So early Saturday morning

This is the way we go to church
Go to church, go to church
This is the way we go to church
So early Sunday morning

Here We Go Round the Mulberry Bush - Historian R.S. Duncan claims this popular nursery rhyme was a song first sung by the female prisoners at Wakefield Prison in Yorkshire. Duncan was a former warden at the prison and wrote a book where he described, a mulberry tree in the outdoor area of the women's prison where the prisoners were taken to exercise.

PLAY IS SELF-CHOSEN AND SELF-DIRECTED

FIVE ELEMENTS OF PLAY
(GRAY, 2013)

ONE

PLAY IS DRIVEN BY THE DESIRE OF THE PLAYER OR PLAYERS. IT IS WHAT THEY WANT TO DO, NOT WHAT THEY ARE BEING TOLD TO DO OR FEEL OBLIGED TO DO. PLAYERS SET THE RULES FOR THEIR PLAY NOT ONLY DECIDING WHAT IT IS THEY WANT TO PLAY, BUT ALSO HOW THEY ARE GOING TO PLAY IT AND OFTEN WHO THEY ARE GOING TO PLAY IT WITH. IN PLAY THAT INVOLVES MORE THAN ONE PLAYER, DOMINANT PERSONALITIES MAY APPEAR TO LEAD THE PLAY. THIS IS ONLY WITH THE AGREEMENT OF THE OTHER PLAYERS (OFTEN NON-VERBAL) AND THAT DOMINANCE CAN SHIFT FREELY BETWEEN PARTICIPANTS AS THE PLAY EVOLVES AND PROGRESSES.

THERE IS USUALLY A SIGNIFICANT ELEMENT OF JUSTICE AND FAIRNESS IN PLAY. RULES CAN BE INVENTED BY ANY OF THE PLAYERS BUT MUST BE AGREED BY ALL — EVEN IF THOSE RULES THEN CHANGE AS THE GAME MOVES ON. AS CHILDREN PLAY BECAUSE THEY ARE MOTIVATED, NOT OBLIGED TO DO SO, THEY CAN LEAVE THE GAME AT ANY POINT. IF THE PLAY CEASES TO BE ADVANTAGEOUS, MOTIVATING OR FAIR ANY PLAYER CAN WALK AWAY AND/OR ESTABLISH A NEW PLAY FOCUS.

FOR MORE ON THE FIVE ELEMENTS OF PLAY, GO TO APRIL 4

The construction area makes me feel happy and excited. I love building bat caves.

TEDDY, AGE 5

'The true
object of all
human life
is play.'

▷ ▷ ▷ G. K. Chesterton

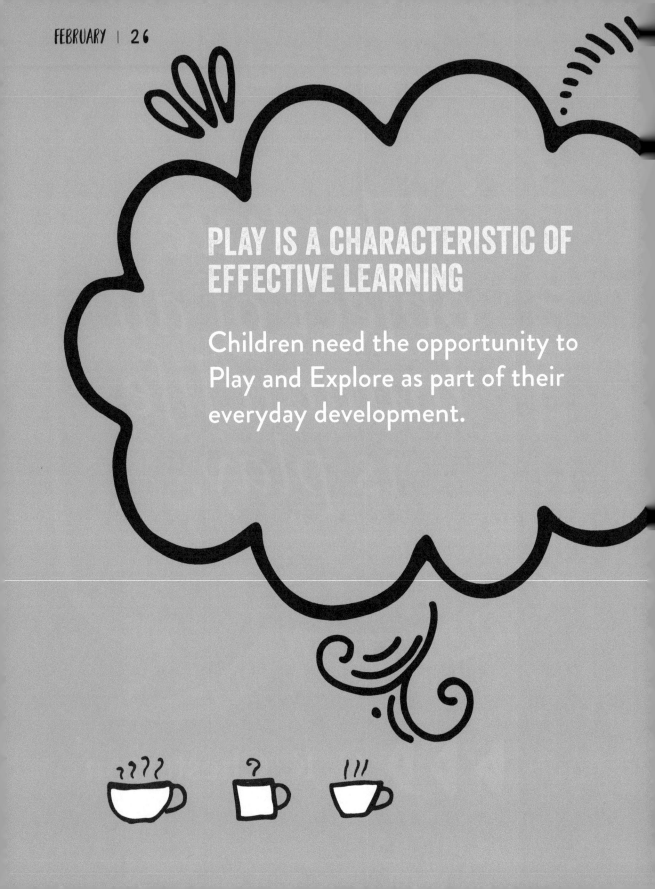

PLAY IS A CHARACTERISTIC OF EFFECTIVE LEARNING

Children need the opportunity to Play and Explore as part of their everyday development.

EMPATHY IS ONE OF THE HARDEST SKILLS FOR SOME YOUNG CHILDREN TO MASTER

It is very difficult to put yourself in someone else's shoes when your own shoes don't quite fit yet!

Play is an excellent vehicle to facilitate this.

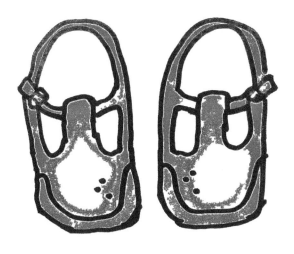

FOCUSING THEIR ATTENTION

OUTDOOR PLAY CAN INCREASE ATTENTION SPAN. TIME SPENT IN UNSTRUCTURED PLAY OUTDOORS IS ENGAGING FOR LOTS OF CHILDREN AND THEREFORE FOCUSES THEIR ATTENTION. OFTEN MORE SUCCESSFULLY THAN INDOOR ACTIVITIES!

DEVELOP
CO-ORDINATION

SKILL

THROUGH PLAY CHILDREN CAN...

DEVELOP CO-ORDINATION
THROUGH FASTENINGS ON
CLOTHES, POURING TEA FROM
TEA POTS, SETTING TABLES,
DRESSING DOLLS.

FRIEDRICH FROEBEL (1782–1852)

Froebel was a huge influence on attitudes to Early Childhood education in the 18th century and he still is on our practice today. He is also the man who founded the Kindergarten. He made a clear link between learning and children's drive to be curious. He called this their 'activity drive'.

'Because I find that one of the basic causes of defective childcare is the unsatisfactory consideration of the activity drive of the child, I have endeavoured to create an institution for this very purpose. An institution under the motto: "Come let us live with our children."

These games not only nourish the inner activity drive, but they also teach the use of the child's immediate environment as a means for play and occupation and as educational aids. They are games and occupations, ways and means, which give a presentiment of the connection between human life and nature. Finally, games which are educative and developing for the person who plays with the children, which influence him and in their alternating educational function become a genuine bond between them both.'

In this quote from Froebel, you can clearly see many of the principles of Early Education that remain unchanged today. He was a thinker ahead of his time!

STAGES OF PLAY
STAGE ONE (1)

At this stage, children play only with realistic toys and show no interest in object substitution performed by adults.

For more on stages of play, go to May 18

' A child loves his play, not because it's easy, but because it's hard. '

▷ ▷ ▷ Benjamin Spock

I like making models in the construction area. I like making cars with roofs that come down. I feel happy.

KIAN, AGE 4

IMAGINARY GUESTS

3 years old is often the time when an extra 'imaginary' guest moves into your house or setting for a while!

You will have to leave them a space on the carpet, help to get them dressed, make sure they see the story book and wait while their every word is interpreted through your child.

This is an IMPORTANT STAGE of play development for some children, but not all. 3-year-olds will begin to experiment with acting out lots of roles, often simultaneously. They will change their characters and their story lines in quick succession.

WE ABSOLUTELY SHOULD CREATE BEAUTIFUL AND INSPIRING SPACES FOR OUR CHILDREN TO PLAY AND LEARN IN. SPACES THAT MOTIVATE THEM, ENCOURAGE THEM TO BE CREATIVE AND CRITICAL THINKERS AND ALLOW THEM TO EXPLORE THE WORLD AROUND THEM THROUGH PLAY.
- ALISTAIR BRYCE-CLEGG

Play nicely girls...

In 1861 a man named Herbert Spencer wrote a book called '*Education, Intellectual, Moral and Physical*'. Herbert had been greatly influenced by the work of Charles Darwin and his theory of evolution, which had caused a great deal of uproar in the society of the time. He very much argues that learning would be far more successful if it was made as pleasurable as play but doesn't go so far as to link the two ideas together.

He does however comment on the fact that girls were prevented from engaging in noisy play by their schools whilst it was positively encouraged for the development of boys!

PLAY IS NOT A BREAK FROM LEARNING. IT IS ENDLESS, DELIGHTFUL, DEEP, ENGAGING, PRACTICAL LEARNING. IT'S THE DOORWAY INTO THE CHILD'S HEART!

— VINCE GOWMON

Rock-a-bye baby

Rock-a-bye, baby, in the treetop
When the wind blows, the cradle will rock
When the bough breaks, the cradle will fall
And down will come baby, cradle and all

Rock-a-bye Baby - Thought to be about the belief that King James II tried to pass off a baby that wasn't his as his son. The story goes that the King had a child brought into the castle to be the Catholic heir to the throne.

The wind blowing in the rhyme is meant to represent the breath of people whispering about their growing suspicions of the King's plan. The bough breaking and the baby falling at the end of the song represent the secret being broken and the Kingdom finding out about James' plan.

RiSK HEROES

Experience Risk

IF CHILDREN DON'T GET THE
CHANCE TO EXPERIENCE
RISK THROUGH PLAY THEN
THEY WILL HAVE TO LEARN WHEN IT IS
HAPPENING FOR REAL AND THAT CAN HAVE FAR MORE
DEVASTATING CONSEQUENCES FOR EVERYONE CONCERNED.

The National Institute for Play describes seven play patterns:

- ATTUNEMENT PLAY, which establishes a connection, such as between newborn and mother.
- BODY PLAY, in which an infant explores the ways in which his or her body works and interacts with the world, such as making funny sounds or discovering what happens in a fall.
- OBJECT PLAY, such as playing with toys, banging pots and pans, handling physical things in ways that use curiosity.
- SOCIAL PLAY, play which involves others in activities such as tumbling, making faces, and building connections with another child or group of children.
- IMAGINATIVE OR PRETEND PLAY, in which a child invents scenarios from his or her imagination and acts within them as a form of play, such as princess or pirate play.
- STORYTELLING PLAY, the play of learning and language that develops intellect, such as a parent reading aloud to a child, or a child retelling the story in his or her own words.
- CREATIVE PLAY, by which one plays with imagination to transcend what is known in the current state, to create a higher state. _For example_, a person might experiment to find a new way to use a musical instrument, thereby taking that form of music to a higher plane; or, as Einstein was known to do, a person might wonder about things which are not yet known and play with unproven ideas as a bridge to the discovery of new knowledge.

AT 3 AND 4 YEARS OLD...

Children are making sense of the world that they are experiencing, especially in relation to social interactions and re-enactment of first-hand experiences. We can support them in this development by enhancing their play with familiar resources that support the children to rehearse and revisit.

'SAFE' DANGER

WRESTLING, CHASING, PLAY FIGHTING ALL HELP CHILDREN TO EXPERIENCE 'SAFE' DANGER, ASSESS RISK AND TAKE APPROPRIATE ACTION. AS A SPECIES WE ARE 'HUNTER GATHERERS'. MUCH OF THE WAY THAT CHILDREN PLAY IS GROUNDED IN INSTINCT AND AN INNATE DESIRE TO HONE OUR SURVIVAL SKILLS. OUR EXPERIENCE OF CURRENT CULTURE JUST DRESSES THEM DIFFERENTLY FROM OUR DAYS IN THE CAVE!

ALISTAIR BRYCE-CLEGG

'*Play fosters belonging and encourages cooperation.*'

▷ ▷ ▷ Stuart Brown

INTERACTING AND SOCIALISING

For a (REAL) quality play experience you need to provide lots of opportunities for social interaction and objects that will promote open ended play.

What is crucial is that the children have lots of opportunities to interact and socialise, that their imaginations can run wild and take a leap.

IT IS SPACE AND TIME THAT UNDERPIN THE FUNDAMENTAL PRINCIPLES OF QUALITY PLAY.

We play cus we
have to share
with everyone.

ABDULELAH, AGE 4

SIGMUND FREUD (1856–1939)

Freud's name is well known and associated with the world of psychology. As interest in how the psychology of adults affected their behaviour, there was also growing interest into the psychology that underpinned the behaviour of children. Freud had a number of theories and methods of expressing his thinking, some of which have become central to how we understand children's emotional development and link to how we support them in approaching their play development.

Freud proposed that from birth to 12 months all babies are dominated by unconscious urges for instinctual self-gratification, which he named the 'Id'.

Through a series of experiences where babies attempt and fail they reach a more realistic idea of what it is possible to achieve, this Freud called the 'Ego'.

As they grow older and move from babies to children, they begin to recognise and portray their parents' views and values of the world, subconsciously following their rules and regulations. This subconscious compliance he called the 'Super-Ego'. These are the basis for developing a conscious.

Freud also proposed that a child went through five stages of development, these he linked to sexual energy:

The Oral Stage – birth to 12 months
The Anal Stage – 12 to 36 months
The Phallic Stage – 36 months to 5/6 years of age
The Latency Stage – 5/6 years to puberty
The Genital Stage – Puberty to adulthood

Whilst some of Freud's thinking has gone on to be disproved, he is still influential in the development of children and their play as his idea of putting what we know about children into stages of development was used by many other theorists as a starting point for their work.

SENSORY MOTOR ACTIONS

SKILL

THROUGH PLAY CHILDREN CAN . . .

DEVELOP THEIR SENSORY AND MOTOR SKILLS. CHILDREN MAKE SENSE OF THE WORLD THROUGH THEIR SENSES AND PHYSICAL ACTIONS.

'*Play has been man's most useful preoccupation.*'

▷ ▷ ▷ Frank Caplan

ADULT CONSENT

A NECESSARY CONDITION, THAT BY ITS ABSENCE HAS OCCASIONALLY DISRUPTED THE UNIVERSALITY OF PLAY, IS ADULT CONSENT. CHILDREN'S LACK OF POWER IN RELATION TO ADULTS HAS LED TO THEIR PLAY BEING CURTAILED WHEN ADULTS HAVE DISAPPROVED OF IT.

ALISTAIR BRYCE-CLEGG

I like the big sand pit outside because I like feeling it. It makes me feel pink and love.

DEBRA, AGE 4

'*Children need the freedom and time to play. Play is not a luxury. Play is a necessity.*'

▷ ▷ ▷ Kay Redfield Jamison

CREATIVITY

SKILL

THROUGH PLAY CHILDREN CAN . . . .

EXPRESS THEIR OWN CREATIVE
IDEAS IN AN OPEN
LEARNING SPACE.

I like playing outside. I like being a king with my friends. I'm happy.

AAL-E-MUHAMMED, AGE 5

' *People tend to forget that play is serious.* '

▷ ▷ ▷ David Hockney

PRACTITIONER NOTE

ADAPTABILITY:

If you want children to be able to experience, consolidate and then practise all of the skills that play can offer then 'adaptability' is the key. If you are over themed or over prescriptive in your provision then you are significantly reducing learning opportunities.

What motivates one child in their play does not always motivate another. So why would thirty children all be motivated by the same thing?

YOU LEARN MORE EFFECTIVELY THROUGH SOME HEALTHY COMPETITION

OFTEN WHEN YOU PLAY (BE IT SPORTS, BOARD GAMES OR AN OFFICE COMPETITION), THERE IS A BIT OF HEALTHY COMPETITION IN THERE. AS LONG AS THE COMPETITION IS ONE OF CHILDLIKE INNOCENCE (RATHER THAN CONQUER AND CRUSH), IT BOOSTS YOUR HAPPINESS LEVELS AS WELL AS YOUR PERFORMANCE. IT CAN ALSO STRENGTHEN THE BOND YOU HAVE WITH THE PEOPLE YOU PLAY WITH.

ALISTAIR
BRYCE-CLEGG

CREATIVITY

PLAYING OUTDOORS STIMULATES CREATIVITY. ROCKS, STONES AND MUD PRESENT LIMITLESS OPPORTUNITIES FOR PLAY.

CHILDREN CAN FIND DIFFERENT INTERPRETATIONS OF THE SAME OBJECTS EVERY TIME THEY STEP OUTSIDE.

EDUCATION AND PLAY

INCREASINGLY, THESE TWO THINGS HAVE BECOME TO BE SEEN AS SEPARATE ENTITIES. PLAY IS SOMETHING THAT YOU DO WHEN YOU ARE 'LITTLE' AND THEN YOU GO TO 'SCHOOL' TO LEARN. FOR CENTURIES BEFORE SCHOOLS WERE EVEN INVENTED CHILDREN (AND A HOST OF OTHER ANIMALS) LEARNED WHAT THEY NEEDED TO KNOW THROUGH SOCIAL INTERACTIONS AND PLAY. TO PLAY IS INTRINSICALLY HUMAN AND TO LEARN TO BE HUMAN WE NEED THE OPPORTUNITIES TO PLAY AND PLENTY OF THEM. THE MOST IMPORTANT ASPECTS OF OUR EDUCATION OCCUR DURING OUR PLAYFUL INTERACTIONS. THE TWO ARE ONE IN THE SAME.

ALISTAIR
BRYCE-CLEGG

DO NOT KEEP CHILDREN TO THEIR STUDIES BY COMPULSION BUT BY PLAY.

– PLATO

PLAY IS INTRINSICALLY MOTIVATED — MEANS ARE MORE VALUED THAN ENDS

FIVE ELEMENTS OF PLAY
(GRAY, 2013)

PLAY OFTEN DOES NOT START OUT WITH A PLANNED END GOAL, ALTHOUGH THE PLAY MIGHT HAVE A THEME OR A FOCUS, THE ACTUAL CONTENT OF THE PLAY HAS YET TO UNFOLD. PLAY IS FACILITATED FOR THE SAKE OF PLAYING, NOT BECAUSE THERE IS A REWARD OR END GOAL.

WHEN IN PLAY, THE PLAYERS ARE FOCUSED ON PROCESS MAPPING AND BUILDING THE ROUTE AS THEY GO.

PLAYERS WILL SET AND ACHIEVE GOALS AS PART OF THE PLAY PROCESS. ONCE A GOAL HAS BEEN ACHIEVED THEN THE PLAY WILL MOVE FORWARD OR END. PLAY CAN OF COURSE BE COMPETITIVE. BUT IN COMPETITIVE PLAY IT IS THE PROCESS OF HOW YOU WIN THAT IS IMPORTANT RATHER THAN JUST THE WIN ITSELF. THAT IS WHAT MAKES THE DIFFERENCE BETWEEN COMPETITIVE PLAY AND A COMPETITION.

ENGAGING IN PLAY CAN LEAD TO LONG-TERM BENEFITS FOR CHILDREN IN A RANGE OF AREAS FOR DEVELOPMENT, BUT FOR THE PLAYERS, PLAY IS DONE FOR ITS OWN SAKE IN THE SHORT TERM, NOT FOR THE LONG-TERM BENEFITS THAT IT MIGHT PRODUCE.

FOR MORE ON THE FIVE ELEMENTS OF PLAY, GO TO JUNE 8

I like making a big plane outside with my friends. I love being the pilot and flying the plane to Disney Land. It's lots of fun and I feel really happy.

NAOMI, AGE 5

A WORLD WE DO NOT YET KNOW

THE MODERN WORLD CAN BE A TRICKY PLACE FOR THOSE OF US THAT INHABIT IT, AND IT IS CHANGING - FAST. IT (REALLY) IS NOT THAT LONG AGO THAT I WAS POPPING TO THE PHONE BOX ACROSS THE ROAD WITH LOTS OF 2P'S SO THAT I COULD PHONE MY GRANNY WHO LIVED UP THE ROAD. NOW I COULD NOT ONLY SPEAK TO HER, BUT ALSO SEE HER FOR FREE EVEN IF SHE WAS ON THE OTHER SIDE OF THE WORLD!

THE WORLD THAT OUR CHILDREN INHABIT NOW, IS NOT THE SAME WORLD THAT THEY WILL INHABIT AS ADULTS. MOVING FORWARD OUR CHILDREN ARE GOING TO NEED TO BE MORE RESILIENT AND CREATIVE THAN EVER. WHILST WE CANNOT PREPARE THEM FOR EVERY ASPECT OF A WORLD THAT WE DO NOT KNOW, WHAT WE CAN DO IS EQUIP THEM WITH A RANGE OF SKILLS AND ATTITUDES THAT THEY CAN APPLY TO ANY AND EVERY SITUATION THAT THEY COME ACROSS.

AND THE **BEST WAY** TO DO THAT? PLAY!

ALISTAIR BRYCE-CLEGG

CARING FOR THE PLANET

Playing outdoors is a great way to give children an appreciation of the environment they live in. The better their understanding, the more likely they are to go on to protect and enhance it.

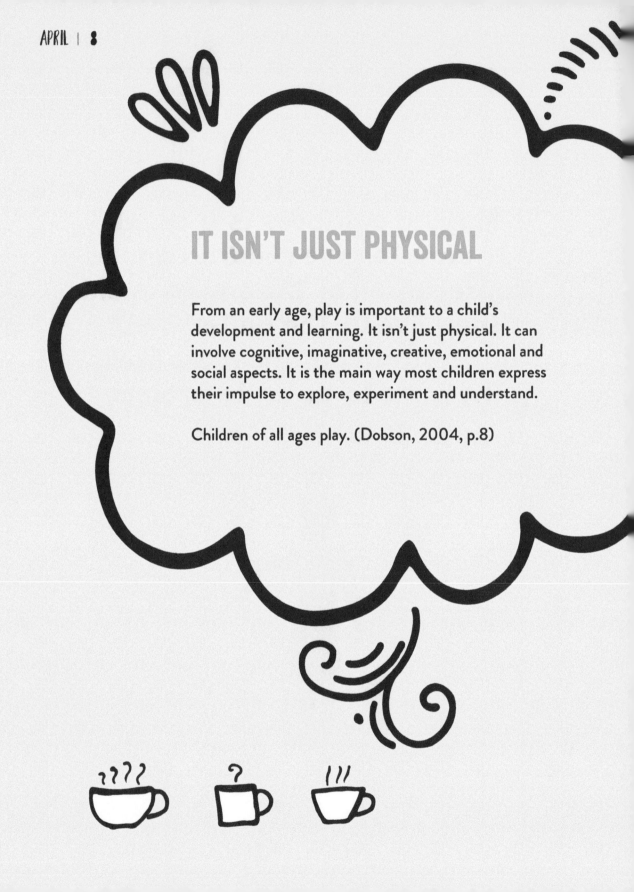

IT ISN'T JUST PHYSICAL

From an early age, play is important to a child's development and learning. It isn't just physical. It can involve cognitive, imaginative, creative, emotional and social aspects. It is the main way most children express their impulse to explore, experiment and understand.

Children of all ages play. (Dobson, 2004, p.8)

' *Deep meaning lies often in childish play.* '

 Johann Friedrich von Schiller

RECEPTIVE AND EXPRESSIVE LANGUAGE

SKILL

THROUGH PLAY CHILDREN CAN . . .

DEVELOP THEIR USE OF RECEPTIVE AND EXPRESSIVE LANGUAGE. CHILDREN LEARN TO LISTEN TO AND UNDERSTAND WHAT IS BEING SAID TO THEM. THEY DEVELOP THEIR ABILITY TO COMMUNICATE THEIR IDEAS AND THOUGHTS IN A WAY THAT OTHERS CAN UNDERSTAND.

TAKE A BACK SEAT

The BEST way to ★ENCOURAGE★ a child to initiate their own learning is for the adult to remain in the background, supporting the individual's natural curiosity and offering helpful ways to

explore their play.

SOCIAL INTERACTION...

increases the speed and accuracy of children's learning.

So the more opportunities to play together the better!

RUDOLPH STEINER
(1821–1925)

Steiner moved our thinking around children's play and learning forward with his theory that children learn by observing the adults around them. They take on the behaviours that they observe, some consciously and some subconsciously. Steiner also proposed that children not only copy the physical actions of the adults around them but also take on their beliefs and values. Relationships between children and adults are key to Steiner's philosophy. Children need to be in an environment where time is given for those quality relationships to develop through interaction and play.

Steiner put a huge emphasis on play and creative arts in children's early development. He also believed it was important for children to engage with their natural world. When it comes to reading and writing, Steiner felt that children would develop these skills naturally if their levels of well-being were high, so these skills weren't introduced until later on in their education. Instead children were encouraged to develop their imagination and creativity. Steiner is also famous for the Steiner-Waldorf schools that he set up on the invitation of Emil Molt who owned the Waldorf Historia cigarette factory. He wanted the children of his workers to be educated, hence the Steiner school movement began.

THE LANGUAGE OF PLAY

Play brings unity across the World. You don't have to speak someone's language to play with them. Play bridges gaps that language can't.

'*Man is most nearly himself when he achieves the seriousness of a child at play.*'

▷ ▷ ▷ **Heraclitus**

Indoors and outdoors

Play takes place indoors and outdoors and it is in these different and often diverse environments that children explore and discover their immediate world. They can practise new ideas and skills, they take risks, show imagination and solve problems on their own or with others.

The role that adults have is crucial. Adults provide time and space and appropriate resources to enable children's play. Adults can discover a huge amount about a child by watching and listening to their play.

PHYSICAL DEVELOPMENT

SKILL

THROUGH PLAY CHILDREN CAN . . .

DEVELOP FINE MOTOR SKILLS AND CO-ORDINATION THROUGH MANIPULATING REAL TOOLS SUCH AS WHISKS, TELEPHONES AND KEYBOARDS.

WHAT IS PLAY?

Play allows children to practise, imagine and rehearse problems and possibilities before they happen. Lots of opportunity to do this will equip children not with the solutions to every eventuality they will come up against, but the strategies for problem solving and a wealth of experience to draw upon. Role playing with other children not only reinforces social interactions but gives of the children involved the opportunity to learn about the thoughts, reactions and strategies of others, which will in turn enhance their own.

PRACTITIONER NOTE

ASSESSMENT

There are a huge number of things that can easily be assessed by observing children in play from the more obvious and apparent assessment of vocabulary and language structure to the more subtle aspects of child development like confidence and schema.

Emotional development through play

Susan Isaacs was a pioneer of children's play putting the development of emotions and feelings at the heart of her practice. She was committed to children using play to solve the problems that they encountered in their everyday lives. She based a lot of her thinking on careful observation of children at play and was keen to point out how different children's needs were at each stage of their development. She encouraged practitioners to be aware of this development and provide an environment that was rich in resources to meet the needs of the children playing within it.

Through her writing she outlines many of the common behaviours in children that we would now refer to as schematic play and recognises the importance of children being able to move and handle a variety of objects not only to facilitate imaginative play, but also real, practical problem solving.
So much of what we know and do in Early Years today is thanks to the work and play of Susan Isaacs.

"If we were asked to mention one supreme psychological need of the young child, the answer would have to be 'play' – the opportunity for free play in all its various forms. Play is the child's means of living and of understanding life."
The Educational Value of a Nursery School Susan Isaacs 1937

1) PHYSICAL – both gross and fine motor

2) COGNITIVE – becoming a thinker and a problem solver

3) SOCIAL AND EMOTIONAL – understanding your own and others' feelings

4) COMMUNICATION – both verbal and non-verbal. All of these can be effectively developed through opportunities to play.

I like making things especially making pictures for my mum which makes her happy.

LUKE, AGE 5

MARIA MONTESSORI
(1870–1952)

Montessori is one of the most recognised names in the field of Early Childhood education with many settings and practitioners referring to themselves as 'Montessori'. There is no doubt that her thinking and her pioneering work has had a huge impact on how we approach children's play and learning today.

Montessori created a theory of child development that was based on the stages that a child goes through as they are learning. She called these stages 'planes'. It was Montessori's observations of children at play that led her to create this system of observation and assessment.

At the core of Montessori's thinking is the idea that children are individuals and should be supported to develop at their own pace. This development is underpinned with opportunities for children to become self-sufficient and independent which enables them to be less reliant on adults and more able to facilitate their own learning.

A great deal of Montessori's work and thinking can be seen in the many curriculums and frameworks for children in the Early Years across the world.

COMMITMENT

Children show a great level of commitment to things that interest them.

' *Children at play are not playing about. Their games should be seen as their most serious minded activity.* '

 Michel de Montaigne

ENVIRONMENT AND EMOTIONS

Helen Bilton, author of 'Playing Outside' describes one of the benefits of outdoor play.

The environment where we work and play affects our emotions. Children will often be less inhibited outside, and more willing to join in with activities, talk and come out of their shells. In overcrowded spaces children's behaviour can change, some can become more aggressive, while others become more solitary.

For more from Helen Bilton see the 16th of February and 12th of July

THE CREATION OF SOMETHING NEW IS NOT ACCOMPLISHED BY THE INTELLECT BUT BY THE PLAY INSTINCT.

– CARL JUNG

YOU DEVELOP SOCIAL SKILLS WHEN LEARNING THROUGH PLAY

WHETHER YOU'RE PLAYING IN A TEAM STRATEGISING HOW TO MAKE YOUR BEST PLAY, OR WHETHER YOU'RE PLAYING ONE-TO-ONE, YOU DEVELOP YOUR SOCIAL SKILLS THROUGH PLAY. YOU LEARN TO TALK TO YOURSELF IN A MORE POSITIVE, MOTIVATING MANNER, AS WELL AS MORE EFFECTIVELY COMMUNICATE WITH OTHERS. SIMPLY BEING WITH OTHERS WHEN PLAYING, AND WATCHING HOW OTHERS APPROACH THE SAME GAME, IS A LEARNING EXPERIENCE IN ITSELF.

ALISTAIR BRYCE-CLEGG

THEORY OF MIND

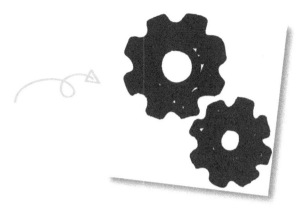

'Theory of mind' is the ability to understand that others have thoughts and feelings all of their own. Young children are very aware of their own thoughts and feelings but often show little or no recognition that others may be experiencing similar emotions. Lots of opportunities to play with other children really help to support this development.

UNSTRUCTURED OUTDOOR PLAY

IN MORE UNSTRUCTURED OUTDOOR PLAY, CHILDREN HAVE MORE OPPORTUNITIES FOR PRACTICAL PROBLEM SOLVING. APPLYING WHAT THEY KNOW IN REAL-LIFE SITUATIONS AND EVALUATING THE OUTCOMES ARE IMPORTANT AND EFFECTIVE STRATEGIES FOR LIFE.

COUNTERING GENDER STEREOTYPES

In chapter 6 of *Challenging Gender Stereotypes in Education*, Maria Kambouri-Danos discusses the importance of countering gender stereotypes through careful consideration of play provision in early years settings:

It is important for professionals working with young children to think about how different areas of play provision can be set up and used to counter gender stereotypes.

For example, the kind of materials provided in the 'home corner' will affect the context the children will choose for their play and the roles that they will act out. When choosing the materials, it is important to make gender neutral choices (texture, colours, themes) and involve the children in the process of selecting these materials to ensure all children will be interested in playing.

JOHN DEWEY (1859–1952)

John Dewey was an American-born educationalist whose thinking was very radical for its time. He was an advocate for a child-centred approach to learning, believing that what a child experienced both in and outside of their school or setting had a significant impact on what and how they learned. Dewey suggested that teachers spent a significant amount of time getting to know the individual preferences and experiences of their pupils.

They could then go on to specifically shape the learning they provided to the needs of the child. He promoted the idea of a varied curriculum where children's interests would help shape the curriculum.

For Dewey the role of the adult was seen as facilitator for learning tailored to the children as opposed to someone who delivers the same learning to all of the children in the same way. He was very aware that children's curiosity was a driving force for their motivation to learn and the more unique the learning to be to them, the more curious they would be and the more success they would have.

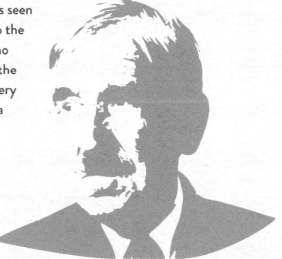

PLAY KEEPS US VITAL AND ALIVE. IT GIVES US AN ENTHUSIASM FOR LIFE THAT IS IRREPLACEABLE. WITHOUT IT, LIFE JUST DOESN'T TASTE GOOD

— LUCIA CAPOCCHIONE

'Necessity may be the mother of invention, but play is certainly the father.'

▷ ▷ ▷ Roger von Oech

This Little Piggy

This little piggy went to market.
This little piggy stayed at home.
This little piggy had roast beef
But this little piggy had none.
And this little piggy went
"Wee wee wee"
All the way home

This Little Piggy Went to Market – Tradition will tell us that this nursery rhyme details the selling of pigs at the market. Farmers would go through different routines in order to get their pigs ready for sale, such as feeding them beef to make them fatter for eating and breeding and even not feeding them at all to ensure that when they are brought to market, there is a smaller chance of them bringing a disease.

All of these different ideas feature in this rhyme. If the pigs weren't sold then that was bad news for the farmer, hence 'this little piggy' squealing, all the way home.

I Blame the Victorians...

The Victorians were really keen on formal schooling and in 1880 made it compulsory for all children to go to school. They also thought that learning would be done best in silence, sitting still for long periods of time. Play only happened at designated 'playtimes'. It was certainly not seen as a means of learning. If this approach to learning wasn't for you, then systematic humiliation and harsh physical punishment seemed to be the order of the day. It wasn't until 1986 that the UK banned this type of punishment in the state sector. Even though corporal punishment has thankfully gone, there are a remarkable number of Victorian principles of education that still exist in our schools today.

The Victorians did not have access to the information that we have about how our brains develop and what sort of learning is appropriate at each stage of a child's development.

They wanted to achieve:

Standardisation
Linearity
Control
Conformity
Compliance

I would argue that to equip our children for the society of tomorrow it is far more important that they have:

Creativity
Ingenuity
Mental Agility
Adaptability
Sociability

A play-based approach to learning will tick all of those boxes and a great deal more!

WHAT IS PLAY?

Any spontaneous or organised activity that provides enjoyment, entertainment, amusement or diversion. It is essential in childhood for the development of a normal personality and as a means for physical, intellectual, and social development. Play provides an outlet for releasing tension and stress, as well as a means for testing and experimenting with new or fearful roles or situations. (Mosby's Medical Dictionary, 2009)

Extraordinary improvisers

Children have no set or fixed plan for how their play will develop. The scenario emerges as a result of the children's interactions.

'*Play keeps us fit physically and mentally.*'

▷ ▷ ▷ Stuart Brown

CONSIDER YOUR OWN VALUES AND POSITION WHEN IT COMES TO PLAY

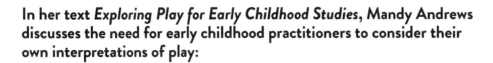

In her text *Exploring Play for Early Childhood Studies*, Mandy Andrews discusses the need for early childhood practitioners to consider their own interpretations of play:

'All early childhood practitioners should take time to observe children at play and consider how play and playful activity is seen through behaviours of children. This would mean beginning not with theoretical definitions of play, or policy statements about the benefits of play, but with a consideration of what children are actually doing when we consider them to be 'at play'. Undertaking your own observations and reflections at this point will help you to define play and consider your own values and position in relation to the term.'

PRACTITIONER NOTE

Quality play encourages...

children to revisit, explore and expand their learning experiences. The more comfortable they are in the play spaces you create, the more effective their learning will be.

I like playing with the boxes because I like making dens with them. I like making dens because I can play mums and dads and it makes me feel happy.

ARLO, AGE 5

IT'S NEVER JUST A BOX

IT IS WORTH REMEMBERING THAT A CARDBOARD BOX IS NEVER JUST A CARDBOARD BOX WHEN IT IS IN THE PLAY OF A CHILD WITH EVEN JUST A LITTLE BIT OF IMAGINATION.

ALISTAIR BRYCE-CLEGG

WHEN CHILDREN PRETEND THEY'RE USING THEIR IMAGINATIONS TO MOVE BEYOND THE BOUNDS OF REALITY. A STICK CAN BE A MAGIC WAND. A SOCK CAN BE A PUPPET. A SMALL CHILD CAN BE A SUPERHERO.
— FRED ROGERS

THE 12 INDICATORS OF PLAY

1. USING FIRST-HAND EXPERIENCES
2. MAKING UP RULES
3. MAKING PROPS
4. CHOOSING TO PLAY
5. REHEARSING THE FUTURE
6. PRETENDING
7. PLAYING ALONE
8. PLAYING TOGETHER
9. HAVING A PERSONAL AGENDA
10. BEING DEEPLY INVOLVED
11. TRYING OUT RECENT LEARNING
12. COORDINATING IDEAS, FEELINGS AND RELATIONSHIPS FOR FREE-FLOW PLAY

STAGES OF PLAY
STAGE ONE (2)

Children at this stage demonstrate a very early realisation that they can 'pretend'. Through play they can create familiar actions and scenarios that they are revisiting based on experience.

For more on stages of play, go to May 30

Opportunities for discussion

Outdoor play should offer the opportunity for children to initiate and take part in games that encourage them to engage in personal interactions, conversations, negotiation and often conflict resolution.

BURRHUS SKINNER (1904—1990)

Burrhus Skinner was interested in human behaviour. He was fascinated by children's behaviour and how adults respond to it can impact on learning. Skinner was an advocate of active learning. In many education systems the children would be passive learners expected to sit and listen to instruction or learn by repetition any information that was chosen by the teacher. Skinner felt that if students could become involved in their learning then their levels of interest would rise. This in turn would result in more engagement and that engagement would result in success. This would then motivate the children to want to learn more and also comply with their learning and behaviours.

Skinner felt that teachers needed to be taught about the science of behaviour and learning rather than just what to teach. If they understood 'how' their students learn then they would be better able to provide a curriculum that was linked to success rather than falling back on old teaching habits that often don't work.

Skinner's theories were underpinned by the concept of positive reinforcement and the impact that has on children's well-being.

We see Skinner's influence in our Early Years settings today where adults are very aware of the stages of development and are able to motivate children and extend their learning through play-based engagement.

'In play a child always behaves beyond his average age, above his daily behavior. In play it is as though he were a head taller than himself.'

▷ ▷ ▷ Lev Vygotsky

RISK

Through physical 'crash and bang' style play children get the opportunity in a controlled, safe and supportive environment to explore what is impossible and dangerous and experience cause and effect in relation to their actions. They can take 'safe' risks which will ultimately help them to take more calculated risks in the real world. They can create and explore simulated realities without having to change what is happening in their own 'real worlds'.

MORE IMAGINATIVE FANTASY GRADUALLY EMERGES IN THE PRETEND PLAY OF TWOS.

Two-year-olds sometimes lose sight of the line between fantasy and reality - even in their own pretending.

TRYING AND TESTING OUT LIFE

PLAY IS A SAFE GROUND FOR TRYING AND TESTING OUT LIFE WITHOUT THREATENING CHILDREN'S PHYSICAL OR EMOTIONAL WELL-BEING, CHILDREN FEEL SAFE BECAUSE THEY KNOW THAT THEY ARE PLAYING. EVEN THOUGH CHILDREN SHOW A GREAT CAPACITY FOR BEING ABLE TO SUSPEND THEIR DISBELIEF AND BECOME COMPLETELY ABSORBED IN THE ROLES THAT THEY ARE PLAYING, THEY STILL KNOW THAT THEY ARE IN PLAY.

ALISTAIR BRYCE-CLEGG

DISPOSITION

PERSISTENCE

PLAY BUILDS PERSISTENCE. COMMITMENT TO THEIR PLAY DRIVES CHILDREN TO COMPLETE SELF-CHOSEN TASKS

PRACTITIONER NOTE

Spontaneity

Much of group play, by its very nature, involves making it up as you go along. As there is no prescribed pathway or script children have more opportunity for spontaneity. This often also has an impact on their creativity and they have complete freedom to do and say whatever comes into their heads.

A CHILD'S GREATEST ACHIEVEMENTS ARE POSSIBLE IN PLAY.

LEV S. VYGOTSKY

London Bridge is Falling Down

London Bridge is falling down
Falling down, falling down
London Bridge is falling down
My fair lady

Build it up with iron bars
Iron bars, iron bars
Build it up with iron bars
My fair lady

Iron bars will bend and break
Bend and break, bend and break
Iron bars will bend and break
My fair lady

Build it up with gold and silver
Gold and silver, gold and silver
Build it up with gold and silver
My fair lady

London Bridge is falling down
Falling down, falling down
London Bridge is falling down
My fair lady

London Bridge is Falling Down - This rhyme is supposedly describing the 1014 attack on Britain by the Viking King, Olaf II, however, some people think the attack never happened and the tune was created by the Vikings, as a PR exercise, so they could intentionally spread it around Europe to make themselves seem more fierce!

STAGES OF PLAY

STAGE ONE (3)

In this initial stage of play, children tend to act, talk, and dress like people they know. They will use real objects as props in their play. There is a high, almost exclusive element of reality in their play. For instance, a child may pick up a spoon and pretend to feed a doll or teddy bear. They may pick up a phone and mimic talking to their mother or father. Children start to develop a concept of a 'pretended role' but need to ground that with the actual props that are used. This play is most often a solitary activity.

For more on stages of play,
go to July 4

I like to build dens because I like dens and I build them with boxes or tables. It makes me feel like I'm going to go in the den and find something.

HENRY, AGE 4

WHAT DOES CURIOSITY LOOK LIKE?

In chapter 1 of _A Broad and Balanced Curriculum in Primary Schools_, Kate Thorpe considers this question:

Perhaps it's about providing opportunities for children to explore and manipulate materials and mediums in new and innovative ways?

Perhaps it's about stimulating reasoning; making connections; discovering how and why things work, are designed; awakening an understanding of the reciprocal nature of the world. . .

Early years teachers can scaffold and facilitate critical thinking and reflection – through providing an environment with resources and questions that invite the child to be creative and curious.

A CONSTELLATION

PETER GRAY TALKS ABOUT PLAY NOT NEATLY DEFINED IN TERMS OF ANY SINGLE CHARACTERISTIC; INSTEAD, IT INVOLVES A CONSTELLATION OF CHARACTERISTICS. I LOVE THE USE OF 'CONSTELLATION' AS IT REPRESENTS AN INFINITE NUMBER OF POSSIBILITIES DEPENDING ON WHO THE PLAYER IS. NOTHING SAYS UNIQUENESS MORE THAN THAT.

ALISTAIR
BRYCE-CLEGG

DEVELOPING THE SKILLS TO USE SYMBOLIC ACTIONS AS COMMUNICATION

In play, children imagine how something might 'be' or 'feel' and then use this as a mechanism for their play.

Actions can speak louder than words

'*The opposite of play is not work. It's depression.*'

▷ ▷ ▷ **Brian Sutton-Smith**

JEAN PIAGET (1896-1980)

Piaget's studies as a Professor of Child Psychology lead him to think about the patterns of learning and thinking that children have at different stages in their lives.

Piaget theorised that young children understand new information better when they have had more of a chance to interact with the world around them. He suggested that by learning about their environment, young children could build up their own knowledge and understanding of new ideas because they learn how to build mental pictures. Piaget called these mental pictures 'schema'.

He later took this theory further by suggesting that children's learning followed 4 stages. These stages are the sensorimotor stage (0-2 years), the preoperational stage (2-7 years), the concrete operational stage (7-11 years) and the formal operational stage (11-15 years). He saw these stages as important because he believed that teachers should give children tasks that are stimulating and appropriate for the stage they are in. Later on in his life, Piaget saw that children develop at different rates and thought that his stages may have been slightly too rigid. Piaget's theories are very different from a lot of the ideas of many behaviourists that came before him. He suggested that children should be encouraged to discover the world around them instead of letting new information come to them from their environment. Piaget's theories were received well at the time and still influence Early Years practice today.

MATURITY CONSISTS IN HAVING REDISCOVERED THE SERIOUSNESS ONE HAD AS A CHILD AT PLAY.

— FRIEDRICH NIETZSCHE

PLAY IS GUIDED BY MENTAL RULES, BUT THE RULES LEAVE ROOM FOR CREATIVITY

FIVE ELEMENTS OF PLAY

(GRAY, 2013)

THREE

ALTHOUGH CHILDREN ARE FREE TO ENGAGE IN PLAY, THE PLAY ITSELF IS NOT FREE OF STRUCTURE. PLAY ALWAYS HAS STRUCTURE, AND THAT STRUCTURE DERIVES FROM RULES IN THE PLAYERS' MINDS. IN SOCIAL PLAY, THE RULES MUST BE SHARED, OR AT LEAST PARTIALLY SHARED, BY ALL OF THE PLAYERS. THE RULE-BASED NATURE OF PLAY IS THE CHARACTERISTIC THAT VYGOTSKY (1978) EMPHASIZED MOST STRONGLY, AS HE BUILT HIS ARGUMENT THAT PLAY IS THE MEANS BY WHICH CHILDREN LEARN TO CONTROL THEIR IMPULSES AND ABIDE BY SOCIALLY AGREED-UPON RULES.

THE RULE-BASED NATURE OF PLAY IS AN EXTENSION OF THE POINT MADE ABOVE ABOUT THE PROMINENCE OF MEANS IN PLAY. THE RULES OF PLAY ARE THE MEANS. THE RULES ARE NOT LIKE RULES OF PHYSICS, NOR LIKE BIOLOGICAL INSTINCTS, WHICH ARE AUTOMATICALLY FOLLOWED. RATHER, THEY ARE MENTAL CONCEPTS THAT OFTEN REQUIRE CONSCIOUS EFFORT TO KEEP IN MIND AND TO FOLLOW. THE RULES OF PLAY PROVIDE BOUNDARIES WITHIN WHICH THE ACTIONS MUST OCCUR, BUT THEY DO NOT PRECISELY DICTATE EACH ACTION; THEY ALWAYS LEAVE ROOM FOR CREATIVITY. ACTIVITIES THAT ARE PRECISELY PRESCRIBED BY RULES ARE BETTER REFERRED TO AS RITUALS RATHER THAN AS PLAY.

DIFFERENT TYPES OF PLAY HAVE DIFFERENT TYPES OF RULES. A BASIC RULE OF CONSTRUCTIVE PLAY, FOR EXAMPLE, IS THAT YOU MUST WORK WITH THE CHOSEN MEDIUM IN A MANNER AIMED AT PRODUCING OR DEPICTING SOME SPECIFIC OBJECT OR DESIGN THAT YOU HAVE IN MIND. IN SOCIODRAMATIC PLAY (THE PLAYFUL ACTING OUT OF ROLES OR SCENES, AS WHEN CHILDREN PLAY 'HOUSE' OR PRETEND TO BE SUPERHEROES) THE FUNDAMENTAL RULE IS THAT PLAYERS MUST ABIDE BY THEIR SHARED UNDERSTANDING OF THE ROLES THAT THEY ARE PLAYING; THEY MUST STAY IN CHARACTER. EVEN PLAYFUL FIGHTING AND CHASING, WHICH MAY LOOK WILD TO THE OBSERVER, IS CONSTRAINED BY RULES. AN ALWAYS-PRESENT RULE IN CHILDREN'S PLAY FIGHTING, FOR EXAMPLE, IS THAT THE PLAYERS MIMIC SOME OF THE ACTIONS OF SERIOUS FIGHTING, BUT DON'T REALLY HURT THE OTHER PERSON. THEY DON'T HIT WITH ALL THEIR FORCE (AT LEAST NOT IF THEY ARE THE STRONGER OF THE TWO); DON'T KICK, BITE, OR SCRATCH. BECAUSE OF ITS RULE-BASED NATURE, PLAY IS ALWAYS AN EXERCISE IN SELF-RESTRAINT.

FOR MORE ON THE FIVE ELEMENTS OF PLAY, GO TO AUGUST 18

Playing with my friends outside makes my heart feel happy. I like playing scary dinosaurs. Roar!!! I don't get scared. It's just pretend.

MIKAELA, AGE 3 (USA)

EXTENDED LANGUAGE EXPERIENCES

Play can be used really effectively to extend children's vocabulary and language use. The key to success here is the role of the other adult (or in some cases, peer). When children are engaged in an exciting play experience, they can only use the language that they know already.

New language is not going to spring into their head like magic. So engaging play scenarios are essential to extend the language mechanisms and the vocabulary that children are using and then share new and exciting language that will take that learning forward.

BRAIN DEVELOPMENT

Play including talking, singing, reading and exploring objects and the physical space is the best way to stimulate brain development.

JOINT PLANNING AND COGNITIVE STRATEGIES

In play, children work together to come up with a plan. Through their play, children are building valuable skills.

CHILD DEVELOPMENT
3-4 YEARS

Around the age of three, play is often related to their real-life experiences. It will usually involve interaction with others and often includes props and lots of language.

SUCCESSFUL SPACES

SUCCESSFUL PLAY SPACES ARE GOOD PLACES FOR SOCIAL INTERACTIONS ALLOWING CHILDREN TO CHOOSE WHETHER AND WHEN TO PLAY ALONE OR WITH OTHERS, TO NEGOTIATE, COOPERATE, COMPETE AND RESOLVE CONFLICTS.

THE TRULY GREAT ADVANCES OF THIS GENERATION WILL BE MADE BY THOSE WHO CAN MAKE OUTRAGEOUS CONNECTIONS, AND ONLY A MIND WHICH KNOWS HOW TO PLAY CAN DO THAT.

– NAGLE JACKSON

BUILDING PERSONAL, SOCIAL AND EMOTIONAL SKILLS

DURING GROUP PLAY, CHILDREN CAN CO-OPERATE, TAKE TURNS AND INITIATE ROLE-PLAY.

PRACTITIONER NOTE

Although you might have in your head what you think children's responses will be to the environment and play opportunities that you provide, be prepared to go with whatever they come up with, remembering that ALL of the children do not think the same as each other, never mind you!

DISPOSITION

REFLECTIVITY

THINKING ABOUT
AND SHARING THEIR
EXPERIENCES THROUGH
PLAY ENABLES CHILDREN
TO REFLECT ON THEIR OWN
LEARNING

JURI, AGE 4

ASSIGNING ROLES

In the early stages of peer play, one child often assigns roles to the others – who may find creative ways to make up their own.

LEV VYGOTSKY (1896–1934)

Vygotsky's theories are similar to Piaget's as they both suggest that there are 4 stages of development that children go through as they learn. The difference, however, is that Piaget suggested that all children would follow the 4 stages he theorised whereas Vygotsky thought that they would alter depending on the culture the children were learning in.

Vygotsky spent his life in the oppressive soviet regime and this influenced a lot of his theories. He believed that things like nursery rhymes, folk tales, etc. were all 'cultural tools' that affected how children learn as they moulded the children's perception of the world around them. Modern day 'cultural tools' would be television, film and the Internet.

He suggested that these 'cultural tools' and play together were integral parts of young children's learning because communication is an important component of how children learn. He theorised that children are born with the foundation for thinking and it is communication that allows them to develop this foundation into a higher level of thinking.

Through play, Vygotsky thought that children gained independence, which meant they would take more individual risks and learn more about their environment which would set them up to be more successful learners in the future when they reached formal education.

Despite having similar ideas, Vygotsky placed much more emphasis on the importance of language, play and communication compared to Piaget. Vygotsky was less interested in the fundamental nature of children's learning and more interested in the cultural contexts that children grow up in.

RISK HEROES

Superhero Play

PROVIDES POSITIVE SYMBOLS OF POWER THAT CHILDREN CAN TAKE ON, FOR THE VAST MAJORITY OF CHILDREN DAY-TO-DAY LIFE OFFERS NO OTHER EXPERIENCE LIKE THIS.

PRACTITIONER NOTE

The truth is that you can only recognise what you already know. The more you improve your own knowledge about how children learn the more you will be able to support them. The best way to do that is when you observe them in play.

PLAY IS THE HIGHEST EXPRESSION OF HUMAN DEVELOPMENT IN CHILDHOOD, FOR IT ALONE IS THE FREE EXPRESSION OF WHAT IS IN A CHILD'S SOUL.
– FRIEDRICH FROEBEL

NOBODY PUTS WRITING IN A CORNER

In his book *Can I Go and Play Now?*, Greg Bottrill discusses the importance of signalling to children that writing is everywhere.

Writing frames and resources should be everywhere in your play space. Lined paper, boxes, folded sheets, mini books, big books, use your imagination. Think what you could use for children to write on **as part of their play**. If writing resources need dressing up then dress them up. Make sure you have well-resourced mini writing tables around your play space, not just a 'writing corner'. A sole writing corner looks lovely but it can send out the message that this is the only place children can write in. You are trying to encourage writing as something that is done anywhere and everywhere, inside and outside and part of play.

RISK

When risky play is not permitted, children lose out on developing key skills as a player. They also pick up very negative messages around education and how their own preferences, needs and desires fit in with our education agenda as adults. These negative messages are likely to affect their engagement in learning full stop. Children who have their starting points for play blocked at an early age may not achieve their potential because they do not feel positive about themselves as learners.

WHAT IS PLAY?

Vygotsky characterised children's play as activity that is:

Desired by the child
Always involves an imaginary situation
Always involves rules (which are in the minds of the players
and may or may not be laid down in advance)

IMPLICIT RULES

SKILL

THROUGH PLAY CHILDREN CAN . . .

LEARN ABOUT MORE COMPLEX AND SUBTLE RULES THAT EXIST WITH PLAY LIKE ENGAGING OTHERS IN THEIR PLAY AND MAINTAINING FANTASY PLAY, EVEN THOUGH THEY KNOW THAT IT IS NOT 'REAL'.

SOCIAL SIGNALLING

Play is crucial to our social development. It helps us to become familiar with our own preferences and feelings as well as learn to recognise the emotional state of others. A lack of play opportunities means that we do not get the opportunity to observe, practise and rehearse the subtleties of social signalling which make us effective and appropriate communicators.

THE PLAYING ADULT STEPS SIDEWARD INTO ANOTHER REALITY; THE PLAYING CHILD ADVANCES FORWARD TO NEW STAGES OF MASTERY.

- ERIK H. ERIKSON

I love looking for worms under the logs. They feel squirmy and soft. I like looking at the worms wiggle. It makes me laugh when they fall off my hand!

IAN, AGE 3 (USA)

' *It is becoming increasingly clear through research on the brain, as well as in other areas of study, that childhood needs play. Play acts as a forward feed mechanism into courageous, creative, rigorous thinking in adulthood.* '

 Tina Bruce

SPACES

CHILDREN SHOULD BE ABLE TO PLAY, EXPLORE, INVESTIGATE AND INTERPRET IN WAYS THAT ARE PERSONAL TO THEM. UNIQUE CHILDREN REQUIRE UNIQUE SPACES.

STAGES OF PLAY

STAGE TWO (1)

In this stage, children automatically imitate adult-initiated object substitutions, but do not appear to understand that one object has been substituted for other. E.g. adult uses a banana as a phone, child copies the action in play with the adult.

For more on stages of play, go to August 8

'*Children learn as they play. Most importantly, in play children learn how to learn.*'

▷ ▷ ▷ O. Fred Donaldson

WEAPONS

WHATEVER YOU CALL IT, 'ROUGH', 'SUPERHERO' OR 'WEAPON PLAY' IS A NECESSARY PART OF CHILDREN'S PLAY AND DEVELOPMENT. IT HELPS THEM TO BUILD AND MAINTAIN APPROPRIATE SOCIAL AWARENESS, COOPERATION, FAIRNESS AND ALTRUISM. IT ALSO ENSURES THAT THEY CAN DISTINGUISH BETWEEN PLAY FIGHTING AND REAL AGGRESSION. ROLE-PLAY FIGHTING IS A COMMON FEATURE OF DEVELOPMENT THE WORLD OVER BOTH IN THE DEVELOPED AND UNDEVELOPED WORLD. IT IS ALSO A FEATURE OF ROLE PLAY THAT IS SHARED BY THE MAJORITY OF THE ANIMAL KINGDOM. CONTRARY TO POPULAR BELIEF IT IS NOT A PRECURSOR TO VIOLENT BEHAVIOUR, IN FACT THERE IS AN ARGUMENT THAT IF CHILDREN WERE GIVEN MORE ACCESS TO PLAY FIGHTING THEN THE INSTANCES OF 'REAL' FIGHTING WOULD BE SIGNIFICANTLY LESS.

CHILDREN OFTEN HAVE A VERY NATURAL DESIRE FOR POWER AND CONTROL. ALTHOUGH WE MAY GIVE CHILDREN A RANGE OF CHOICES WITHIN THEIR EVERYDAY ROUTINES, WE RARELY ALLOW THEM FULL CONTROL OF WHAT THEY WANT TO DO AND HOW THEY WANT TO DO IT.

ALBERT BANDURA (1925–PRESENT)

Like many before him, Bandura challenged the thinking of the time regarding education and learning. Despite living in a more socially free society (Alberta, Canada), Bandura believed that social factors are key in understanding how children learn, much like Vygotsky.

In his studies, Bandura found that children will mimic the behaviour of others even if there is no reward for doing so, which challenged the theories of philosophers like Freud. His central theory was that children imitate those around them and through their imitations, gain knowledge that they can apply to existing concepts in their head. This led Bandura to stress the importance of children having environments and adults around them that help their learning the most.

Bandura also recognised that children all have different levels of self-belief. Children who have less self-belief won't attempt to complete tasks that they don't think they will be successful within. In the long term, this means that the children with lower self-belief won't do as well as the children who have higher self-belief.

His solution to this is surrounding those children with environments that encourage them to try different, challenging tasks and not to be scared of not succeeding.

Bandura definitely challenged the practice of the time with his theories and built on the ideas of Bruner, Vygotsky and Montessori. The accepted ideas of the time focussed on the best rewards to help children learn, Bandura suggested that there are innate parts of children's learning that do not rely on rewards and stimuli.

PLAY IS A TRICKY CONCEPT

In her text *Exploring Play for Early Childhood Studies*, Mandy Andrews discuss how play is such a difficult concept to define:

'Play is such a common experience that we all think we know exactly what it is. Our own childhood memories may be full of examples of playing: those long hot summer days in the garden; playing with sand on the beach; or perhaps being indoors with small toys spread out on the floor in winter time. I recall my own children playing with my neighbour's children. They created fantasy play adventures around a climbing frame; messed about with water in the summer; created a 'vets' and 'cooked perfume' with mud and grass.

Our use of the term 'play' is so familiar that we do not even stop and think about what it really is, or what we really mean when we use the word. Yet we seem to recognise that there is a common, shared value in it. There is something about 'play' that we all relate to, but actually fail to define. Janet Moyles says that "Grappling with the concept of play can be analogised to trying to seize bubbles, for every time there appears to be something to hold on to its ephemeral nature disallows it being grasped!" (Moyles, 1994:5).'

DISPOSITION

CONFIDENCE

PLAY PROVIDES OPPORTUNITIES FOR CHILDREN TO MAKE THEIR OWN DECISIONS, INCREASING THEIR CONFIDENCE

'*Creative play is like a spring that bubbles up from deep within a child.*'

▷ ▷ ▷ Joan Almon

LEARNING THROUGH MOVEMENT

Helen Bilton, author of 'Playing Outside' describes one of the benefits of outdoor play.

Outdoors is the perfect place to learn through movement, which is one of the four vehicles through which children can learn, the others being play, talk and sensory experiences. All of these happen more naturally outside, but with so much space and so many opportunities to move in different ways, the setting supports learning through movement particularly well.

For more from Helen Bilton
see 16th February and 26th April.

INDIVIDUALITY

Through play, children can express their individuality and unique personalities.

CHILD DEVELOPMENT 4-5 YEARS OLD

Play becomes more sophisticated and complex. Children have had more experience of the world around them, so have more knowledge to draw on. The content of children's play is still very much centred on basic relationships and interactions but the setting for that play and the complexity of the storyline and character often becomes much richer.

AN ESSENTIAL ELEMENT TO REALLY GOOD CONTINUOUS PROVISION IS A BIT OF AMBIGUITY AND OPEN-ENDED EXPERIENCE. CHILDREN NEED TO HAVE THE FREEDOM TO INTERPRET THE ENVIRONMENT WE CREATE IN THEIR OWN WAY.

— ALISTAIR BRYCE-CLEGG

LISTENING SKILLS

PLAYING OUTSIDE CAN IMPROVE CHILDREN'S LISTENING SKILLS. AS THEY NEGOTIATE THE RULES OF A GAME THEY HAVE INVENTED, THEY MUST DEVELOP THE SKILL OF LISTENING AS WELL AS TALKING, BE ABLE TO ASK QUESTIONS TO MAKE SURE THEY UNDERSTAND AND LISTEN TO THE DETAILS OF EXPLANATIONS.

REAL LANGUAGE EXPERIENCES

QUALITY PLAY ACTIVITIES PROVIDE CHILDREN WITH THE OPPORTUNITY TO COMMUNICATE IN AUTHENTIC WAYS AND SITUATIONS. THIS HELPS THEM TO REVISIT AND REHEARSE MANY OF THE DAY TO DAY SITUATIONS THAT THEY WILL HAVE COME UP AGAINST IN THEIR EVERYDAY LIVES.

WHEN WE DENY YOUNG CHILDREN PLAY, WE ARE DENYING THEM THE RIGHT TO UNDERSTAND THE WORLD.

– ERIKA CHRISTAKIS

PLAYING ALLOWS CHILDREN TO DEVELOP. . .

a sense of well-being

emotional responses

interpersonal skills

Play involves exploration and creativity. Children think flexibly and become problem solvers.

DISPOSITION

ENTHUSIASM

THROUGH DISCOVERY AND THE OPPORTUNITY TO PURSUE THEIR OWN INTERESTS, PLAY FOSTERS CHILDREN'S ENTHUSIASM

I TRIED TO TEACH MY CHILD WITH BOOKS,
HE GAVE ME ONLY PUZZLED LOOKS.
I TRIED TO TEACH MY CHILD WITH WORDS,
THEY PASSED BY HIM OFTEN UNHEARD.
DESPAIRINGLY, I TURNED ASIDE,
'HOW SHALL I TEACH THIS CHILD,' I CRIED?
INTO MY HAND HE PUT THE KEY,
'COME,' HE SAID, 'PLAY WITH ME.'

– ANONYMOUS

PLAY is a
UNIVERSAL RIGHT
of EVERY child.

(THE UNITED NATIONS CONVENTION ON THE RIGHTS OF THE CHILD)

PRACTITIONER NOTE

MEMORABLE LEARNING EXPERIENCES

It does not matter whether children are using their play to consolidate a home life experience, a fantasy experience or something linked to learning you have facilitated in your setting. The high levels of willing engagement that you get for a well-planned play will usually ensure that some high level attainment takes place. If your play provision is good then children will want to return to it again and again.

MARIA MONTESSORI SAID...

.. that knowing how to arrange an interesting, beautiful environment for children is as much a part of their development as knowing how to select fine children's books for their library.

ABSTRACT THINKING

SKILL

THROUGH PLAY CHILDREN CAN . . . .

THINK ABOUT THE WORLD AROUND THEM IN A DIFFERENT WAY. TO DEVELOP ABSTRACT THINKING SKILLS, CHILDREN NEED TO BE ABLE TO USE AND APPLY THEIR PRIOR KNOWLEDGE UNIQUELY.

WORK CONSISTS OF WHATEVER A BODY IS OBLIGED TO DO. PLAY CONSISTS OF WHATEVER A BODY IS NOT OBLIGED TO DO.

– MARK TWAIN

TIME FOR PLAY

We must give children plenty of room and time for play if we are to see maximum benefits from it. Short periods of playing do not give children the opportunity to play out the scenarios, actions and sequences necessary to really engage the senses, the mind, and their innate creativity. If we allow adequate time and room for these play-based scenarios, then we are supporting the building blocks of learning.

MOVING

OUTDOOR PLAY GETS CHILDREN MOVING AND THIS CAN HELP TO ENSURE THAT THEY HAVE ACTIVE BODIES AND HAVE LESS RISK OF BEING OVERWEIGHT AND UNFIT.

STAFF AT NASA'S JET PROPULSION LABORATORY . . .

take into consideration a person's background of play when they are hiring new scientists. This is because research shows that children who have ample opportunity to play and manipulate the environment creatively, will be the most innovative and original thinkers as adults.

AUGUST

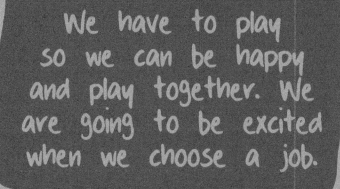

We have to play
so we can be happy
and play together. We
are going to be excited
when we choose a job.

SOPHIE, AGE 4

PLAY IS OFTEN TALKED ABOUT AS IF IT WERE A RELIEF FROM SERIOUS LEARNING BUT FOR CHILDREN PLAY IS SERIOUS LEARNING. PLAY IS REALLY THE WORK OF CHILDHOOD.

- FRED ROGERS

URIE BRONFENBRENNER (1917–2005)

Like Bandura, Bronfenbrenner also provided focus on the importance of a child's environment. Unlike Bandura, Bronfenbrenner's theories focus on a much wider set of factors that could affect a child's learning like economic and social factors. Bronfenbrenner created a model that was meant to represent the level of influence that a child's surroundings had on their learning. At the most influential, he placed the child's immediate surroundings i.e. nursery, family, peers. Bronfenbrenner also pointed out that just as these factors effect the child's learning, the child also has an effect on these factors, much like how Bandura suggested that children all have an effect on the others' learning when in groups.

The next most influential set of factors, according to Bronfenbrenner, is the connections between the factors he had previously named, for example the level of communication between the parents of a child and the nursery they go to or the similarities between a child's class mates and their siblings. Bronfenbrenner points out that from a young age, children will begin to make connections between places like the home and formal education and this will effect how they learn in both places.

Bronfenbrenner then suggests that the social, political and economic influences on the child's parents, playgroup, nursery school, etc. all eventually come to affect a child's learning. Linking to this is the wider cultural context and different world cultures. This theory is heavily inspired by the ideas of Vygotsky. Interestingly, both men spent time living in the USSR's oppressive communist regime. Pointing out the wider culture of a child's learning is also important as that is where folk stories, fairy-tales and children's entertainment are created, building on ideas from Piaget and Vygotsky.

GROSS MOTOR

OUTDOOR PLAY IS OFTEN MORE GROSS MOTOR AND PHYSICAL THAN INDOOR PLAY. CHILDREN PLAYING TOGETHER HAVE OPPORTUNITIES TO ENGAGE IN RULE MAKING, TURN TAKING, SOCIAL INTERACTION AND NEGOTIATION.

IT IS A HAPPY TALENT TO KNOW HOW TO PLAY.

– RALPH WALDO EMERSON

THROUGH PLAY, CHILDREN SHOULD HAVE THE OPPORTUNITY TO DEVELOP CONFIDENCE, SELF-ESTEEM AND SELF-CONTROL IN RE-ENACTING REAL-LIFE SITUATIONS.

SPEAKING OUT LOUD

SPEAKING OUT LOUD IN PLAY ACTIVATES ANOTHER OF THE FIVE SENSES, HEARING. THIS STIMULATION CAN SUPPORT CHILDREN IN THEIR ABILITY TO COOPERATE AND INTERACT WITH OTHERS. IT CAN ALSO ENHANCE THEIR LISTENING SKILLS AND PROBLEM SOLVING ABILITIES.

STAGES OF PLAY

STAGE TWO (2)

In this second stage, children's play is enhanced by their developing imaginations. They are now less dependent on concrete props for role-playing. Children may use a box as a car, or a basket as a hat. The ability to make-believe moves beyond the scope of real props or costumes. Children also learn to use their imaginations to invent actions and situations. At this stage of development we also begin to see the emergence of fantasy that takes the children's play outside of that of their real life experiences. At this stage, children often use such play to help them understand feelings or deal with fears and worries.

For more on stages of play, go to September 2

CHILD DEVELOPMENT

Imaginary friends often appear around the age of

SUCCESSFUL SPACES

SUCCESSFUL PLAY SPACES HELP CHILDREN TO OBSERVE AND APPRECIATE NATURE. TRY PROVIDING PLANTS THAT ENCOURAGE INSECTS, BIRD BOXES AND ANIMALS AS PART OF PROVISION.

YOU CAN DISCOVER MORE ABOUT A PERSON IN AN HOUR OF PLAY THAN A YEAR OF CONVERSATION.

– PLATO

PLAYING TOGETHER, LISTENING, SHARING, TAKING
TURNS, MANAGING A CHANGING SPACE.

A GATEWAY TO COMPLEX LEARNING

WHEN CHILDREN IN A CONTROLLED STUDY WERE GIVEN A TOY THAT DID MULTIPLE THINGS LIKE SQUEAKING AND PLAYING MUSIC, THE CHILDREN WHO WERE SHOWN HOW THE TOY WORKED BY AN ADULT DID NOT EXPLORE IT FURTHER THAN THE DIRECTIONS GIVEN BY THE ADULT.

HOWEVER, THE STUDENTS WHO WERE GIVEN THE TOY WITH NO SPECIFIC INSTRUCTIONS DISCOVERED THE WAY IT WORKED, AS WELL AS SEVERAL DIFFERENT OTHER ASPECTS OF THE TOY THAT WEREN'T IMMEDIATELY OBVIOUS.

THE OPPORTUNITY TO PLAY WITH AND WITHIN THE ENVIRONMENTS OPENS UP A GATEWAY TO COMPLEX LEARNING AND EXPERIENCES.

'A child who does not play is not a child, but the man who does not play has lost forever the child who lived in him.'

Pablo Neruda

PLAY BUILDS THE KIND OF FREE-AND-EASY, TRY-IT-OUT, DO-IT-YOURSELF CHARACTER THAT OUR FUTURE NEEDS.

- JAMES L. HYMES JR.

Play and the immune system

Children having the opportunity to play and interact with the outdoors has shown to have a positive impact on their immune system. As children spend more time outside handling natural objects their immune system improves.

I like to play princesses because they have pretty dresses on. I can put bracelets on and necklaces on and ballgowns.

EMMA, AGE 3 (SINGAPORE)

PLAY IS IMAGINATIVE

FIVE ELEMENTS OF PLAY

FOUR

(GRAY, 2013)

PLAY ALWAYS INVOLVES SOME DEGREE OF MENTAL REMOVAL OF ONESELF FROM THE IMMEDIATELY PRESENT REAL WORLD. THIS IS THE CHARACTERISTIC THAT HUIZINGA (1955) EMPHASISED MOST STRONGLY, AS HE BUILT HIS ARGUMENT THAT PLAY PROVIDES THE ENGINE FOR CULTURAL INNOVATIONS. THIS IS ALSO THE CHARACTERISTIC MOST STRONGLY EMPHASISED BY RESEARCHERS WHO FOCUS ON THE ROLE OF PLAY IN THE DEVELOPMENT OF CREATIVITY AND THE ABILITY TO THINK IN WAYS THAT GO BEYOND THE CONCRETE HERE-AND-NOW. AS VYGOTSKY (1978) POINTED OUT, THE IMAGINATIVE NATURE OF PLAY IS, IN A SENSE, THE FLIP SIDE OF PLAY'S RULE-BASED NATURE. TO THE DEGREE THAT PLAY TAKES PLACE IN AN IMAGINED WORLD, THE PLAYERS' ACTIONS MUST BE GOVERNED BY RULES THAT ARE IN THE MINDS OF THE PLAYERS RATHER THAN BY LAWS OF NATURE OR IMPULSIVE INSTINCTS.

IMAGINATION, OR FANTASY, IS MOST OBVIOUS IN SOCIODRAMATIC PLAY, WHERE THE PLAYERS CREATE THE CHARACTERS AND PLOT, BUT IT IS ALSO PRESENT IN OTHER FORMS OF HUMAN PLAY.

IN ROUGH AND TUMBLE PLAY, THE FIGHT IS A PRETEND ONE, NOT A REAL ONE. IN CONSTRUCTIVE PLAY, THE PLAYERS MAY SAY THAT THEY ARE BUILDING A CASTLE FROM SAND, BUT THEY KNOW IT IS A PRETEND CASTLE, NOT A REAL ONE. IN FORMAL GAMES WITH EXPLICIT RULES, THE PLAYERS MUST ACCEPT AN ALREADY ESTABLISHED FICTIONAL SITUATION THAT PROVIDES THE FOUNDATION FOR THE RULES. FOR EXAMPLE, IN THE REAL WORLD BISHOPS CAN MOVE IN ANY DIRECTION THEY CHOOSE, BUT IN THE FANTASY WORLD OF CHESS THEY CAN MOVE ONLY ON THE DIAGONALS.

FOR MORE ON THE FIVE ELEMENTS OF PLAY, GO TO NOVEMBER 11

THE DEVELOPMENT OF PRETENCE

CHILDREN DEVELOPING THE CAPACITY TO USE THEIR IMAGINATION TO FEED THEIR PLAY.

' *It is in playing, and only in playing, that the individual child or adult is able to be creative and to use the whole personality, and it is only in being creative that the individual discovers the self.* '

 D.W. Winnicott

AN ENVIRONMENT FOR PLAY

OF COURSE, WE WANT CHILDREN TO BE HAPPY – HAPPY CHILDREN MAKE SUCCESSFUL LEARNERS. BUT, WE ALSO WANT CHILDREN TO BE MOTIVATED AND CHALLENGED BY THE RESOURCES THAT WE PROVIDE FOR THEIR PLAY. WE WANT THEM TO BE THINKERS, NEGOTIATORS AND PROBLEM SOLVERS – TO APPLY THE KNOWLEDGE THAT THEY ALREADY HAVE TO ENABLE THEM TO EXPLORE NEW POSSIBILITIES. WHEN YOUR CHILDREN ARE IN FRONT OF YOU AND HANGING ON YOUR EVERY WORD, YOU, THE SKILFUL ADULT CAN IMPART, TEASE AND CELEBRATE KNOWLEDGE AND ACHIEVEMENT. BUT, WHEN THEY GO INTO THEIR OWN PLAY, IT IS THE ENVIRONMENT THAT YOU PROVIDE THAT NEEDS TO DO THAT JOB – ALMOST AS WELL AS YOU DO (AND IN SOME CASES BETTER)!

ALISTAIR BRYCE-CLEGG

Playing alone

Playing is the most effective way for children to learn life skills and find out what they like. Children need opportunities to play alone to explore their thoughts and feelings as well as alongside their peers to rehearse social interactions.

Humpty Dumpty

Humpty Dumpty sat on a wall
Humpty Dumpty had a great fall
All the King's horses and all the King's men
Couldn't put Humpty together again

According to history, Humpty Dumpty wasn't a person (or an egg). It was in fact a huge cannon used by the Royalist Soldiers who were also known as The King's Men during the English Civil War. The cannon was stationed in a castle on top of a big hill to repel attackers. However, when the castle was badly hit in battle, 'Humpty' fell down the hill and was irreparably damaged, despite the best efforts of all the King's horses and all the King's men.

CHILD DEVELOPMENT

Children as young as two know the difference between real and pretend. A two year old might come with an empty cup and offer you a drink of juice. They know there is no juice, they are just enjoying the process of pretend playing. It is important that we provide lots of opportunities for children to explore the wold of real and pretend.

JEROME BRUNER (1915–2016)

Bruner began his career as an American Psychologist and later turned his attention to children's learning. It was his background in psychology that helped him have such an impact on modern day practice. Bruner felt that a lot of the thinking of his time was out-dated and he was passionate about building on the ideas of Freud and Pavlov, among others, to help them fit modern practice.

Like Bandura, Bruner wanted to move away from the idea that children only learn when being presented with stimuli (in other words, a reason to learn about their surroundings). Bruner believed that children had 3 steps for how they learn. The first step is finding new information. The second step is changing and manipulating that information and the third step is checking that information against models that already exist in their heads.

Building on this theory, Bruner came up with 2 fundamental facts. The first fact being that children's knowledge of the world around them is based on the models that they construct within their own head. The second fact is that the models that children construct are adapted from the cultures they live in, similar to the thoughts of Bronfenbrenner, Bandura and Vygotsky.

Bruner also began to think about the idea that children can grow to have different skills from a very young age. He viewed the way of teaching in his time as overly focussed on the range of tasks and stimuli that were provided to children and there was not enough focus on the different ways that different children would solve certain tasks.

It was these early ideas of individual learning and the recognising of the way children gather and apply new information that meant Bruner became a very influential figure in education and now has a great effect on modern practice.

I like playing in the creative area. There's so much stuff and we always make things and that is why I love it so much.

CONSTANTINA, AGE 4

THE WIDER
THE RANGE OF
POSSIBILITIES WE
OFFER CHILDREN,
THE MORE INTENSE
WILL BE THEIR
MOTIVATIONS AND
THE RICHER THEIR
EXPERIENCES.
–LORIS MALAGUZZI

CHILD DEVELOPMENT

Four year olds' play often becomes more sophisticated and will contain a lot of reference to detail.

PLAY BUILDS CONFIDENCE

Play allows children to explore different ideas, project themselves in different ways and get involved in group or team play. All of these things help to raise their confidence and self-esteem.

' *Play gives children a chance to practice what they are learning.* '

▷ ▷ ▷ Fred Rogers

PRACTITIONER NOTE

Revisit the old traditional games like Hop Scotch and ring games.

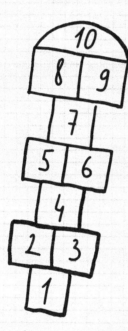

Spend time teaching the children how to play so that they can use them in their own play as well as alongside an adult.

SEPTEMBER

I like building outside. I like building transformers. They are a car and turn into a man. You have to do it with your friends or it will take ages.

LUKE, AGE 5 (UK)

STAGES OF PLAY
STAGE THREE (1)

Children independently imitate object substitutions previously performed by an adult. For example, an adult uses a banana as a phone, the child copies the action in independent play.

For more on stages of play, go to October 12

IN EVERY REAL MAN A CHILD IS HIDDEN THAT WANTS TO PLAY.

- FRIEDRICH NIETZSCHE

PART OF A GROUP

Play supports children to learn how to work as part of a group. In play, children take on different roles, both real-life and imagined.

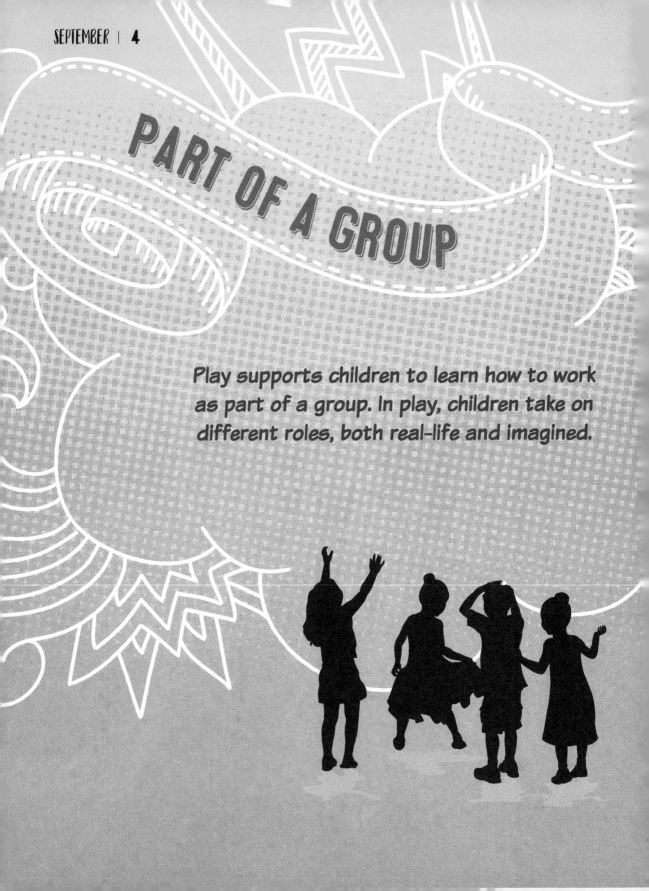

HOWARD GARDENER (1943–PRESENT)

Gardener studied under, and later worked alongside, Bruner and, as a result, a lot of Gardener's theories build on what Bruner had published. As well as Bruner, Gardener also studied with Psychoanalyst Erik Erikson, which explains why his theories are based on the way children's brains work.

For a long time (before Gardener was even born) there has been a debate among philosophers and thinkers about what 'intelligence' is and if it can be measured. Gardener took this question and answered it by creating a list of categories called 'the Multiple Intelligences'.

These categories all reflect skills that a child might represent, for example 'Musical Intelligence' if a child is particularly good at recalling sounds or (later on in their education) recreating music/creating music from scratch or 'Intrapersonal Intelligence' if a child shows a good ability to recognise and express their own feeling or identify someone else's feelings and respond appropriately.

There are 8 categories that Gardener hypothesised children can exhibit talents within. Gardener is also keen to point out that a child shouldn't be confined to just one type of intelligence, for example a child could be good at reading and expressing themselves through writing (Linguistic Intelligence) as well as showing a talent for solving equations, calculations and logical puzzles (Logical-mathematical Intelligence).

His mentor, and later colleague, Bruner began to touch on the idea that children should be treated as having different skill sets and, as a result, their early education should reflect this. Gardener took this further and, by creating his categories of intelligence, gave practitioners and teachers an easier way of identifying these individual strengths. There is little doubt about how big of an influence Gardener had on modern day practice.

RESPECT

SKILL

THROUGH PLAY CHILDREN CAN . . . .

LEARN TO HAVE RESPECT
FOR OTHERS' IDEAS AND
ACCOMMODATE THESE IN ROLE PLAY.

SUCCESSFUL SPACES

SUCCESSFUL PLAY SPACES ALLOW
CHILDREN TO MANIPULATE NATURAL
AND FABRICATED MATERIALS, USE TOOLS,
AND HAVE ACCESS TO BITS AND PIECES
OF ALL KINDS.

A UNIVERSAL TRUTH

That children engage in PLAY seems to be a proposition that is universally true. Whatever historical period is examined, evidence can be found of children playing. The same holds across cultures too, although the content of children's play differs across time and space. Play may also transcend species; the young of many animals also exhibit behaviours that are similar to the play of children.

I love playing with the babies. They are real babies, my teacher told me! So we have to feed them milk, give them cuddles and change their nappies!

HEIDI, AGE 5 (UK)

DEFINITION:

Mihalyi Csikszentmihalyi (1990) called the mental state of play 'flow'. All of the player's attention is on the play itself. They are totally absorbed in how that play will progress and their role within it. They are less aware of the word around them outside of that immediate play as their focus is on the rules, ideas and participants in their play. This absorbed state of being encourages children to be at their most engaged and most creative.

TALK IN THE LANGUAGE OF DIFFERENT ROLES

IN THEIR PLAY, CHILDREN TALK IN THE LANGUAGE OF DIFFERENT ROLES. THESE MAY BE ROLES THAT ARE FAMILIAR TO THEM OR ROLES INVENTED FROM THEIR IMAGINATIONS.

A 'NORMAL' SETTING

SOMETIMES IT CAN BE HARD FOR ADULTS TO SEE OUTDOORS AS AN ENVIRONMENT FOR LEARNING BECAUSE IT IS SO ALIEN FROM WHAT WE PERCEIVE IN EDUCATION TO BE A 'NORMAL' SETTING FOR TEACHING AND LEARNING, BUT OUTDOOR PLAY IS NOT JUST PLAYTIME IT IS A FUNDAMENTAL PART OF CHILDREN'S DEVELOPMENT.

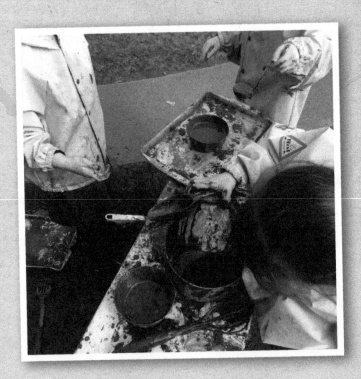

IF YOU WANT TO BE CREATIVE, STAY IN PART A CHILD, WITH THE CREATIVITY AND INVENTION THAT CHARACTERIZES CHILDREN BEFORE THEY ARE DEFORMED BY ADULT SOCIETY.

- JEAN PIAGET

NEGOTIATION

SKILL

THROUGH PLAY CHILDREN CAN . . .

USE LANGUAGE AND
CONVERSATION SKILLS TO REACH
A COMPROMISE OR END RESULT.

A MAN IS GETTING OLD WHEN HE WALKS AROUND A PUDDLE INSTEAD OF THROUGH IT.

– R.C. FERGUSON

CORRE CORRE LA GUARACA

OFTEN THEY ARE SIMPLE GAMES THAT REQUIRE LITTLE OR NO EQUIPMENT WHICH MAKES THEM EASILY ACCESSIBLE AND IMMEDIATE. A LOT OF CHILDREN'S GAMES APPEAR IN SIMILAR FORMS ALL OVER THE WORLD. IF YOU WENT TO CHILE YOU MIGHT PLAY CORRE, CORRE LA GUARACA WHEREAS IN THE UK YOU WOULD CALL IT DUCK, DUCK, GOOSE!

ALISTAIR BRYCE-CLEGG

PRACTITIONER NOTE

CREATE ROLE PLAY

or

SMALL WORLD SITUATIONS

where children can translate their thoughts and feelings through other characters.

That way they do not feel inhibited, embarrassed or judged and are more likely to be receptive to the play.

WORKING INDEPENDENTLY

In play, children learn how to work independently and access the resources they need.

I like to play with the green robots cos they're machines and when you press the button they move.

FREDDIE, AGE 4 (SINGAPORE)

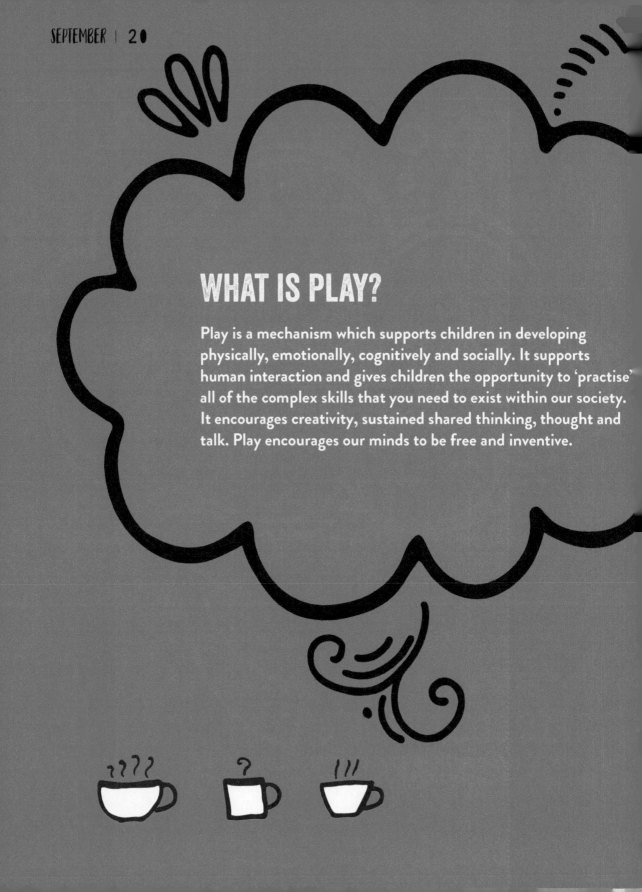

WHAT IS PLAY?

Play is a mechanism which supports children in developing physically, emotionally, cognitively and socially. It supports human interaction and gives children the opportunity to 'practise' all of the complex skills that you need to exist within our society. It encourages creativity, sustained shared thinking, thought and talk. Play encourages our minds to be free and inventive.

WINNING AND LOSING

MANY OF THE GAMES CHILDREN PLAY OUTDOORS HELP THEM TO ENJOY THE FEELING OF WINNING AND MANAGE THE DISAPPOINTMENT OF LOSING. WE NEED TO PROVIDE LOTS OF OPPORTUNITIES FOR CHILDREN TO ENGAGE IN PLANNED AND SPONTANEOUS GAME PLAY.

PROBLEM SOLVING TOGETHER

THROUGH PLAY, CHILDREN LEARN THE JOY OF TAKING TIME TO THINK TOGETHER TO SOLVE A PROBLEM OR ISSUE.

EXPLORING THE WORD 'PLAY'

In her text *Exploring Play for Early Childhood Studies*, Mandy Andrews explores the word 'play':

'The word '*play*' is confusing. It can be a noun, a verb or an adjective. We watch a *play*; musicians *play* their instruments, we can *play* board games and tricks on others, in literature we read of the wind '*playing*' with leaves and children can be '*playful*'. If we delve a little deeper we will find that the word '*play*' has not come from a Latin word for meaningless activity (as we may think!) but actually emerges from an old English word for exercise, or 'brisk movement'. This understanding of '*play*' instantly gives a more positive interpretation to the term than much of its common use. There is indeed energy, movement or action in the concept of *play*. Just as light plays from reflective objects or the wind *plays* with sand and dust, so a child is playing when they are spinning around, with the energy of a 5 year old, experiencing the sheer delight of disorientation. Over time, the wide use of the word play has become synonymous with lightness, pleasure, pastimes without time boundary and a contrast to 'work'.'

I like drawing because I love yellow; yellow paper and yellow pencil. I like to draw my family because I love them.

CLOTHILDE, AGE 4 (SINGAPORE)

CHILD DEVELOPMENT
5-6 YEARS

Children at this age have a strong grasp of the difference between real and pretend. As a result of this you will often see a greater prevalence of more complex fantasy play.

' *Those who play rarely become brittle in the face of stress or lose the healing capacity for humour.* '

▷ ▷ ▷ Stuart Brown, MD

HEROES

Through super hero and weapon type role play...

... CHILDREN CAN LEARN TO MANAGE THEIR OWN FEELINGS BY DISPLACING THEM. THEY CAN MAKE THINGS TURN OUT AS THEY WANT THEM TO, REINVENT THE TRUTH AND EXPLORE OTHER POSSIBLE OUTCOMES THAT WOULDN'T BE POSSIBLE IN 'REAL' LIFE WHERE THERE IS ONLY ONE.

PRACTITIONER NOTE

THROUGH SOMETHING AS
SIMPLE AS

PLAYING

WITH

TOY

BLOCKS

children can translate their
thoughts and feelings through
other characters.

That way they do not feel
inhibited, embarrassed or
judged and are more likely
to be receptive to the play.

PLAY IS THE HIGHEST FORM OF RESEARCH .

– ALBERT EINSTEIN

WHAT IS PLAY?

DUTCH HISTORIAN JOHAN HUIZINGA (1955) SUMMED UP HIS ELABORATE DEFINITION OF PLAY:

Play is a free activity standing quite consciously outside 'ordinary' life as being 'not serious,' but at the same time absorbing the player intensely and utterly. It is an activity connected with no material interest, and no profit can be gained by it. It proceeds within its own proper boundaries of time and space according to fixed rules and in an orderly manner.

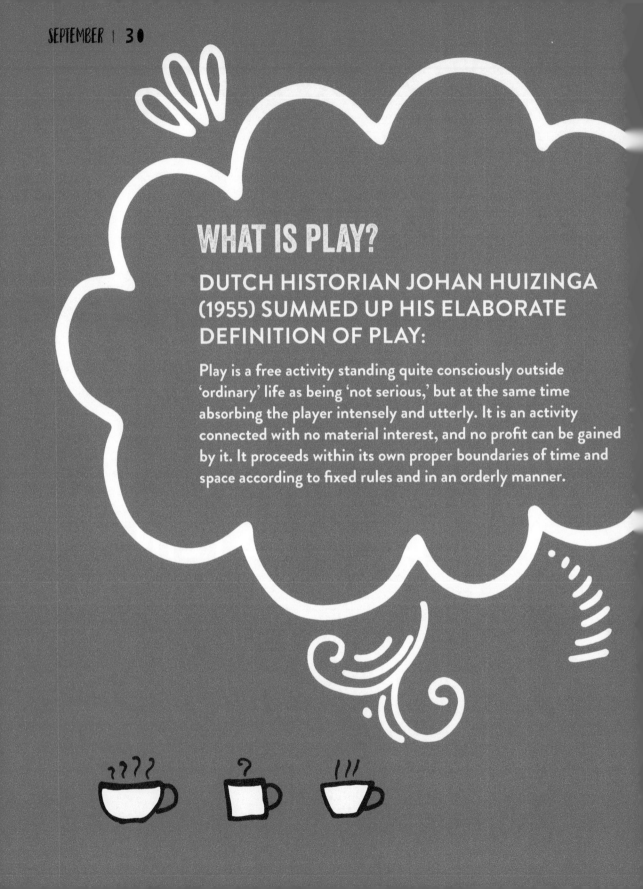

OCTOBER

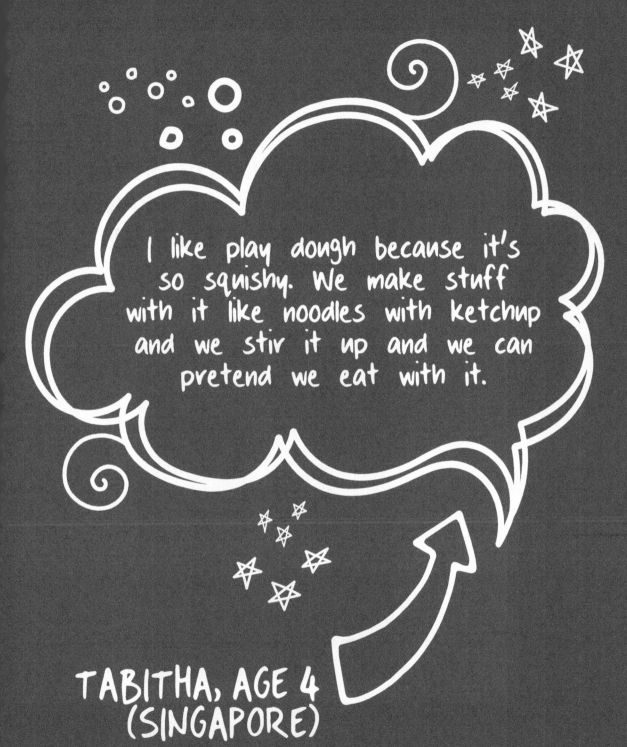

I like play dough because it's so squishy. We make stuff with it like noodles with ketchup and we stir it up and we can pretend we eat with it.

TABITHA, AGE 4 (SINGAPORE)

EMOTIONS

IN A SUCCESSFUL PLAY SPACE, CHILDREN CAN EXPLORE A RANGE OF EMOTIONS IN A SAFE AND SUPPORTED ENVIRONMENT.

Experiences and sensations

The sort of objects, animals, plants, experiences and sensations that children experience in outdoor play opens up a whole new range of opportunities for developing language use and vocabulary.

TEAMWORK

THROUGH PLAY, CHILDREN CAN BUILD TEAMWORK SKILLS. SOMETHING AS SIMPLE AS HELPING TO TIDY UP AT THE END OF A SESSION CAN BE A TEAM ACTIVITY.

REUVEN FEUERSTEIN (1921–2014)

Feuerstein questioned whether intelligence could be measured.

Having lived through World War 2, Feuerstein worked with children who had survived the Holocaust.

When these children were tested academically, they tended to not do very well, however, after working with them on an individual basis, Feuerstein found that they scored much better.

Feuerstein considered whether children have a fixed learning potential and, if not, whether they should be assessed based on their performance or their potential.

After much debate, Feuerstein came to the conclusion that if practitioners view a child's potential to learn as limitless then they can begin to remove barriers that might limit the potential of each individual child.

Feuerstein would encourage teachers to be careful when talking to children about what is expected of them and to use language that suggests that there is nothing that they can't do.

SIMILARITIES AND DIFFERENCES

Playing helps children to notice similarities and differences. The ability to sort items and notice the similarities and differences is an important skill, especially for mathematics. Time outdoors gives children lots of opportunities to categorise, sort and count.

PLAY IS THE WORK OF THE CHILD.

- MARIA MONTESSORI

DENS

In his text *Can I Go and Play Now?*, Greg Bottrill discusses Dens as communication spaces.

Much of the great outdoors will lend itself to communication and the bigger scale you make it the more talk you will potentially enable. Dens however are the opposite.

These small spaces that perhaps only fit two people in are little bubbles of warmth, safety and chat. Make these from whatever resources you wish – tent canvas, wind breaks, plastic storage boxes, pallets, fencing, trellis, branches... the idea is for children to squirrel themselves away.

The best dens are empty other than seating possibly as long as children are able to take resources in with them. These simple communication spaces overflow with language and chat so don't forget to make some of them just about big enough for yourself to get in so you can model and join in the conversation.

NOTHING OTHER

A CHILD CAN PLAY WITH NOTHING OTHER THAN THEIR OWN IMAGINATION. PLAY IS ONE OF THE SIMPLEST AND MOST EFFECTIVE WAYS WE CAN ENABLE OUR CHILDREN TO LEARN

ALISTAIR BRYCE-CLEGG

LEARNING STICKS IN CHILDREN'S BRAINS WHEN IT IS RELEVANT AND MEANINGFUL TO THEM. INFORMATION THAT IS NOT INTERESTING OR NECESSARY LITERALLY GOES IN ONE EAR AND OUT OF THE OTHER.

– ALISTAIR BRYCE–CLEGG

STAGES OF PLAY

STAGE THREE (2)

During this stage of development, socio-dramatic play emerges with children beginning to seek out and enjoy the interaction of playing with others. As more children become involved in the play then the play becomes more complex and lasts for longer periods of time. This sort of play includes elements of real-life play and make-believe play. Unlike the aspects of this sort of play that we have seen in the earlier development of children, this requires social interaction and contribution of two children or more. Because of its interactive nature, this sort of play requires planning. Often the planning can take up as much time as the playing. Because of its more complex story lines, socio-dramatic play requires that children spend a significant amount of time in this type of play.

For more on stages of play, go to October 30

ABDULLAH, AGE 3

LANGUAGE FLUENCY

PRACTISING DIALOGUE AND USING REALISTIC SCENARIOS DURING PLAY WILL ENABLE CHILDREN TO BECOME MORE FLUENT WITH THEIR OWN LANGUAGE AND EXPERIENCE THE LANGUAGE OF OTHERS. PLAYING TOGETHER WILL ALLOW THEM TO PRACTISE WORDS, PHRASES AND SENTENCES IN A REALISTIC SETTING.

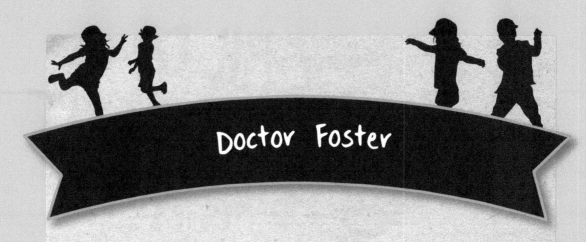

Doctor Foster

Doctor Foster went to Gloucester,
In a shower of rain;
He stepped in a puddle,
Right up to his middle,
And never went there again.

Doctor Foster - This rhyme was written in 1844 about King Edward I who had the nickname Dr Foster. This was because people thought he was very clever and knew he had an interest in medicine. Tradition has it that the rhyme came about from the king mistaking a deep marsh for a puddle on his way into Gloucester. Both him and his horse got stuck in the mud. King Edward was so embarrassed that the town of Gloucester had seen him in this way; he allegedly refused to ever return there!

CHILD DEVELOPMENT 5-6 YEARS

Because the play at this age is often more complex and involved, children will usually stick at it for longer periods of time.

TALKING ABOUT THE WORLD

THROUGH ROLE PLAY SITUATIONS, CHILDREN CAN EXPLORE WHAT DIFFERENT PEOPLE DO, DEVELOPING THEIR LANGUAGE SKILLS AND UNDERSTANDING OF THE WORLD.

LANGUAGE DEVELOPMENT

SKILL

THROUGH PLAY CHILDREN CAN . . .

TALK ABOUT WHAT DIFFERENT PEOPLE DO IN ROLE-PLAY SITUATIONS.

WE DON'T STOP PLAYING BECAUSE WE GROW OLD, WE GROW OLD BECAUSE WE STOP PLAYING.

- GEORGE BERNARD SHAW

PERSONAL, SOCIAL AND EMOTIONAL DEVELOPMENT

SKILL

THROUGH GROUP PLAY
CHILDREN CAN . . .

DURING <u>GROUP</u> PLAY, CHILDREN
CAN CO-OPERATE, <u>TAKE TURNS</u> AND
INITIATE ROLE-PLAY.

LAUGHTER MATTERS

Laughter is a common and important part of children's play. Laughter gives a feeling of security and contentment. Where children feel safe and secure their levels of well-being will be high and that will promote effective learning and development. It is important that we incorporate opportunities for humour into children's play.

Risky Play...

ALLOWS CHILDREN TO EXPLORE QUESTIONS AND EMOTIONS IN A CONTROLLED ENVIRONMENT AND A SAFE CONTEXT. THEY CAN EXPLORE WHAT IS POSSIBLE AND, EQUALLY AS IMPORTANTLY, WHAT IS IMPOSSIBLE. EXPLORING WHAT IS RISKY AND DANGEROUS THROUGH PLAY IS ESSENTIAL IF WE WANT OUR CHILDREN TO BE ABLE TO ACKNOWLEDGE AND ACCEPT THE LIMITS OF REALITY.

AWARENESS OF SPACE

THROUGH PLAY, CHILDREN DEVELOP AN AWARENESS OF THE SPACE AVAILABLE IN THE ROLE-PLAY AREA AND HOW TO SHARE THAT SPACE WITH OTHERS.

THE TYPE OF
COLLABORATIVE PLAY
THAT CHILDREN OFTEN ENGAGE
WITH OUTDOORS IS USEFUL WHEN
IT COMES TO HONING THEIR SOCIAL
SKILLS AS WELL AS THOSE OF...

★ LEADERSHIP

★ NEGOTIATION

★ PLANNING

DISCUSSION.

ALLOWING SPACE FOR NATURAL CURIOSITY

Psychology studies have shown that early learning structured around direct, instructional teaching not only inhibits creativity, but curbs a child's natural curiosity to discover the world around them and how it works.

A successful play-based environment promotes high levels of well-being, engagement and learning.

We play so it
keeps us busy so
we don't get bored.

GEORGE, AGE 4

PLANNING FOR PLAY

Planning for play requires you to plan a high quality learning environment in which children can

- ✧ make choices
- ✧ experiment
- ✧ make connections
- ✧ take risks and
- ✧ independently interact with open ended resources that support all areas of learning and development

McEvoy and McMahon, 2019.

MARK MAKING AND WRITING

SKILL

THROUGH PLAY CHILDREN CAN . .

HAVE THE OPPORTUNITY TO DEVELOP MARK MAKING AND WRITING SKILLS. WHEN MARK MAKING AND WRITING IS PART OF PLAY, CHILDREN ARE MORE MOTIVATED TO TAKE PART.

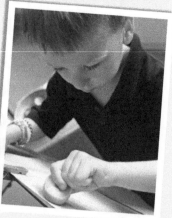

It helps us to find our genius

It brings emotional balance

It helps us to understand body language

It is a fundamental part of being a human being

It is good for mental health

Top 10 Reasons to Play

It generates a feeling of joy

It teaches us patience and self-control

It helps us to problem solve

It keeps your passions alive

It reminds us to communicate

STAGES OF PLAY
STAGE FOUR (1)

In this stage, children select their own substitute objects, but do not rename the objects with substitute names. For example, a child independently selects a wooden brick as a substitute for a phone.

For more on stages of play, go to November 21

DON'T ASSUME PATTERNS OF PLAY AND GENDER

OPPORTUNITIES for play within the environment need to be broad and often ambiguous to meet the needs of all children. Boys are usually more assertive in their interactions and games, girls tend to be more intuitive and relational as they play.

Whilst there are a number of reasons for why this might be the case, it is important that we don't assume patterns of play and gender. We should create a play space for our children shaped by what we have observed about them as unique individuals and not because of their gender.

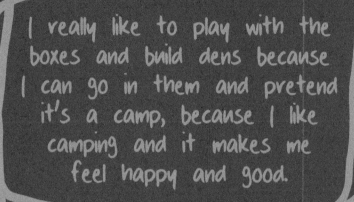

I really like to play with the boxes and build dens because I can go in them and pretend it's a camp, because I like camping and it makes me feel happy and good.

LUKE, AGE 5

DEVELOPMENTAL 'NORMS'

In her text *Childhood in Society*, Rory McDowall Clark discusses the limits of the use of development 'norms' for practitioners:

Childhood professionals are very aware of the developmental 'norms' that are used to measure a child's progress; familiarity with these and the ability to recognise when a child diverges from them is an important skill. Such measures range from the milestones used to check when infants sit up, crawl, walk and say their first word to controversial school tests, which identify children's progress against agreed criteria. Of course, these measures do have a use and familiarity with them is important, but it is also essential to recognise that all norms and standards are culturally specific, and however much we might measure and observe children, this cannot reveal any fundamental 'truths' about childhood. Interpretation of the 'facts' is dependent on the explanations we give them – and that is informed by attitudes and beliefs that have been shaped by social experience.

NEL NODDINGS (1929–PRESENT)

Born in America, Noddings spent the early part of her life as a teacher across the USA. It was through this role that she developed many of the theories that now affect modern practice. Her theories are all centred around what she established as the two types of 'care'.

Her work involved looking at the importance of both the parents and the teachers within the context of a child's learning and how they 'care' for the child in different ways. She thought that teachers care for a child in the respect that they set achievable targets whilst still pushing the child, work hard for them to reach their academic potential and have the child's best interest at the heart of what they do.

She also thought that the parents of the child care for them in a similar yet different way.

Noddings suggests that parents care for their children in a 'relational sense', which means connecting and empathising with the child.

She also points out that these two ways of 'caring' are not mutually exclusive and that children perform best when their parents and practitioners care for them in every sense of the word.

This way of considering the word care and how the adults in a child's learning career can apply it has had a massive impact on modern day attitudes to children's learning.

THROUGH PLAY CHILDREN CAN . . . .

ACQUIRE NEW KNOWLEDGE
THROUGH LANGUAGE, INTERACTION
AND EXPERIENCE.

SUPPORTING CHILDREN TO PLAY REQUIRES US TO REMEMBER WHAT LIFE IS ALL ABOUT. IT'S NOT ABOUT GETTING FROM A-Z, BUT RATHER DREAMING BEYOND BOTH.

- VINCE GOWMON

WHAT IS PLAY?

In her book *Exploring Play for Early Childhood Studies*, Mandy Andrews explores one definition of play:

For some observers play is not an ongoing social activity, but rather is **stimulated by interaction with other people or things** which sets a train of thought, an involvement with materials, or their muscles in motion. The adults, materials or environment rather than direct social interaction or adult involvement may provide the initial stimulus. A parent gives a child a treasure basket (for example) and this stimulates the play activity of exploration in the child. The play element is shown in the responsive behaviour of the child to the materials.

QUESTIONS, QUESTIONS . . .

Children have lots of questions about the world around them, many of which they cannot articulate because they are too subtly attached to emotion. It is these questions that they explore through their play.

I like the house because there's a bed with covers and glass and I party inside.

SANT, AGE 4 (SINGAPORE)

CHILD DEVELOPMENT 5-6 YEARS

A great deal of play will be based around exploring and rehearsing social interaction in a variety of scenarios.

PLAY IS OUR BRAIN'S FAVOURITE WAY OF LEARNING.

— DIANE AKERMAN

AN ACTIVE, ALERT MIND

FIVE ELEMENTS OF PLAY
(GRAY, 2013)

FIVE

PLAY IS CONDUCTED IN AN ALERT, ACTIVE, BUT RELATIVELY NON-STRESSED FRAME OF MIND.

THIS FINAL CHARACTERISTIC OF PLAY FOLLOWS NATURALLY FROM THE OTHER FOUR. BECAUSE PLAY INVOLVES CONSCIOUS CONTROL OF ONE'S OWN BEHAVIOUR, WITH ATTENTION TO MEANS AND RULES, IT REQUIRES AN ACTIVE, ALERT MIND. PLAYERS HAVE TO THINK ACTIVELY ABOUT WHAT THEY ARE DOING. YET, BECAUSE PLAY IS NOT A RESPONSE TO EXTERNAL DEMANDS, AND BECAUSE THE ACTIVITY TAKES PLACE IN A FANTASY WORLD RATHER THAN THE REAL WORLD, AND BECAUSE THE ENDS DO NOT HAVE IMMEDIATE CONSEQUENCES IN THE REAL WORLD, THE PERSON AT PLAY IS RELATIVELY FREE FROM PRESSURE OR STRESS.

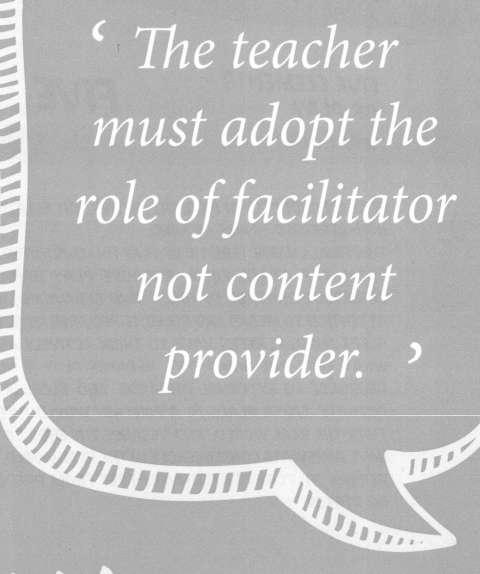

' *The teacher must adopt the role of facilitator not content provider.* '

Lev S. Vygotsky

NOTHING LIGHTS UP A CHILD'S BRAIN LIKE PLAY.

– DR. STUART BROWN

EXPLICIT RULES

SKILL

THROUGH PLAY CHILDREN CAN . . .

LEARN ABOUT <u>EXPLICIT RULES</u>
LIKE <u>PLAYING FAIRLY</u>
AND SHARING.

THE DEBT WE OWE TO THE PLAY OF THE IMAGINATION IS INCALCULABLE.

— CARL JUNG

I love making books about dinosaurs because I just love dinosaurs and it makes me feel happy and so I have lots more books.

LUKE, AGE 5

EXPLORING CULTURE

FOR CHILDREN WITH ENGLISH AS AN ADDITIONAL LANGUE, ENGAGING IN ROLE PLAY WITH OTHER CHILDREN ALLOWS THEM TO EXPERIENCE LANGUAGE IN CONTEXT AND REINFORCES THE LABELING OF FAMILIAR OBJECTS. ENHANCING OUR PLAY SPACES (RATHER THAN OVER THEMING THEM) WITH RESOURCES FROM OTHER CULTURES IS A REALLY EFFECTIVE WAY TO INTRODUCE CHILDREN TO CULTURAL SIMILARITIES AND DIFFERENCES IN A TANGIBLE WAY.

ALISTAIR BRYCE-CLEGG

OBSERVING CHILDREN AT PLAY

In her text *Child Observation*, Ioanna Palaiologou discusses observation as a powerful tool:

Observing children at play is a purposeful and daily reflective method for gathering information about children's behaviour, their needs, experiences and their development. Observation requires a skilful practitioner. Observation is more than just watching children. It requires a set of skills that practitioners need to develop in order to be able to see, *understand* and *act* in their daily practice.

PRACTITIONER NOTE

When teachers have confidence in a child's ability to learn independently, their relationship with the child is stronger. Adults are then able to take a more 'facilitative' role and observe the child who is engaged in active learning. When children are allowed to learn through play, there is far less time spent on behaviour management. A child's attention span is also longer. Play-based learning shifts the focus of learning from the outcome or goal, to the process.

I like playing unicorns because they have magic in their horns. My friend is teaching me how to draw space unicorns.

RUBY, AGE 5

STAGES OF PLAY
STAGE FOUR (2)

Here the child may act out the different roles played by real and fantasy characters that they are familiar with. Unlike a 'play' they will not stick to one role but move between a number of them, shaping the story as they go (very clever!). Through this sort of play children can explore the emotions of different characters and also experience an element of power as they shape the outcomes of their story. The children would normally imitate adult roles and also play alongside adults to expand their experiences.

For more on stages of play, go to December 6

NEGOTIATION SKILLS

THROUGH JOINT DISCUSSIONS THAT LEAD To AN AGREED END RESULT, CHILDREN LEARN NEGOTIATION SKILLS IN PLAY.

FREEDOM AND FOCUS

WHEN THE MIND IS AT PLAY IT IS IN A UNIQUE STATE OF FREEDOM AND FOCUS DRIVEN BY INTEREST AND ENGAGEMENT. THIS STATE OF MIND HAS BEEN SHOWN REPEATEDLY BY PSYCHOLOGISTS TO BE IDEAL FOR LEARNING NEW SKILLS OR MAXIMISING CREATIVITY.

ALISTAIR BRYCE-CLEGG

MENTAL REPRESENTATIONS

SKILL

THROUGH PLAY CHILDREN CAN . . . .

CREATE <u>IDEAS</u> IN THEIR <u>MINDS</u> AND THEN PLAY THEM OUT THROUGH ROLE PLAY.

ENTER INTO CHILDREN'S PLAY AND YOU WILL FIND THE PLACE WHERE THEIR MINDS, HEARTS AND SOULS MEET.

– VIRGINIA AXLINE

SOME BOYS WHO ARE AT RISK OF
BECOMING DISAFFECTED AT A
VERY YOUNG AGE HAVE SHOWN
SIGNIFICANT IMPROVEMENTS IF
THEIR LEARNING TAKES PLACE
OUTSIDE. OPPORTUNITIES WHICH
REFLECT ALL AREAS OF LEARNING
OUTDOORS MUST BE AVAILABLE.

HELEN BILTON

Old Mother Hubbard

Old Mother Hubbard
Went to the cupboard,
To give the poor dog a bone:
When she came there,
The cupboard was bare,
And so the poor dog had none.

Old Mother Hubbard - This nursery rhyme is not about an old mother, or a woman at all! Old Mother Hubbard is thought to be Thomas Wolsey, the Archbishop who first refused Henry VIII a divorce from Catherine of Aragon. This makes King Henry the dog, and his divorce the bone. The peasants of Britain apparently sang this song at the time due to Henry VIII being such an unpopular monarch.

CIVILISATIONS AROUND THE WORLD
HAVE DOCUMENTED THE IMPORTANCE OF PLAY.
VASES AND PLATES FOUND IN ANCIENT GREECE
SHOW IMAGES OF CHILDREN PLAYING. ARCHAEOLOGISTS
HAVE DISCOVERED EXAMPLES OF THE TOYS THAT
ANCIENT GREEK CHILDREN PLAYED WITH.

THEY HAVE DISCOVERED

SWINGS, SEESAWS, KITES, HOOPS WITH BELLS,
GO-CARTS, WHIPPING TOPS AND WHEELS THAT
WERE ATTACHED TO POLES FOR PULLING ALONG.

MANY OF WHICH ARE
STILL POPULAR AROUND
THE WORLD **TODAY.**

PERSISTENCE

Time spent outdoors can increase persistence. Made up games with ever changing rules often require persistence.

Building with natural objects that are not uniform in size and shape also requires persistence. Children are more inclined to keep trying until they are successful if they are motivated by the task.

ROLE PLAY

SKILL

THROUGH PLAY CHILDREN CAN . . . .

SHOW INITIATIVE WHEN DEVELOPING IDEAS. IN THE ROLE-PLAY AREA THEY CAN SHOW THIS BY (FOR EXAMPLE) MAKING SIGNS FOR A SHOP.

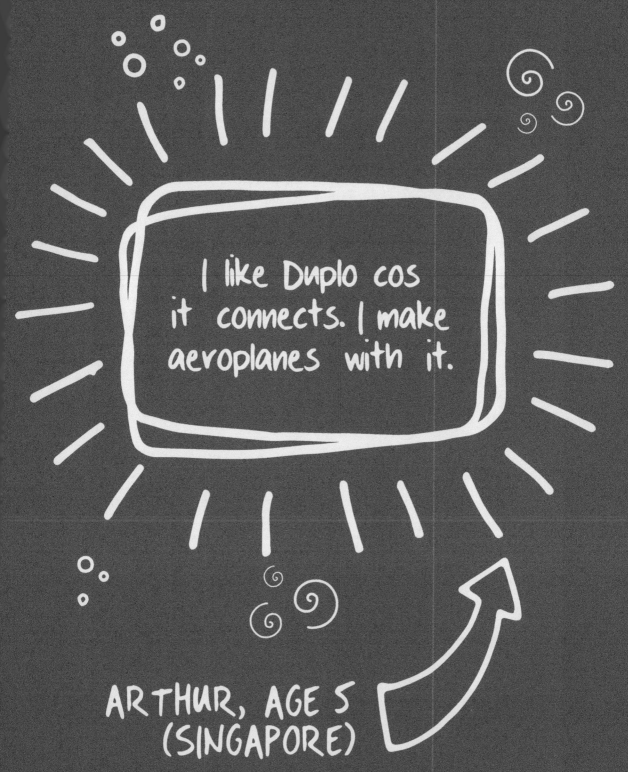

EVERY CHILD IS AN ARTIST. THE PROBLEM IS HOW TO REMAIN AN ARTIST ONCE HE GROWS UP.

- PABLO PICASSO

TE WHÃRIKI (1996–PRESENT)

Te Whãriki is a New Zealand early childhood curriculum first introduced in 1996. It has challenged a lot of the accepted theories of early education and has been very successful. By stressing the importance of feeling like a welcome part of both family and community, it has brought a caring ethos to early years in New Zealand.

The system has 4 main principles:

Empowerment – Giving children the desire to learn and develop both educationally and socially.

Holistic Development – Understanding and overcoming social and emotional barriers.

Family – Developing a sense of belonging within the child's family unit.

Community – Feeling like a valued member of the wider community.

The philosophy of Te Whãriki, which has been adopted by the New Zealand government has 5 over-arching goals.

The first goal is nurturing health with a particular focus on mental health. Practitioners are encouraged to give children the tools to deal with and prevent mental health and well-being issues in the future. The second goal is making sure that the children and their families have a strong sense of belonging in the local and wider communities which contributes heavily to the third aim, which is to treat children as individuals and equals and ensure that they feel like any and all of their contributions are valued. The fourth goal is to advance children's communication.

Many children in Early Years in New Zealand are encouraged to create and practise their own languages as well as developing their verbal and non-verbal communication skills.

Finally, children are encouraged to explore. Explore is used very loosely in Te Whãriki's philosophy as it can be applied to children's emotional well-being, local environment or any other of the structures that they develop from a young age.

MARIA MONTESSORI SAID...

The greatest sign of success for a teacher . . . is to be able to say. 'The children are now working as if I did not exist'.

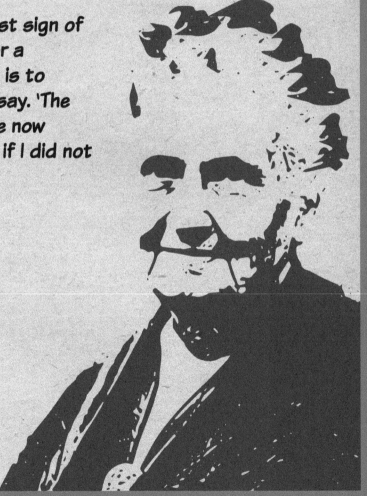

WE ARE NEVER MORE FULLY ALIVE, MORE COMPLETELY OURSELVES, OR MORE DEEPLY ENGROSSED IN ANYTHING, THAN WHEN WE ARE AT PLAY.

- CHARLES E. SCHAEFER

STAGES OF PLAY
STAGE FIVE

Children create unique and fantastical play scenarios. Here the role-playing with peers is paramount and fantasy is often a key element of play.

Children will put themselves into completely fantastic roles like that of an alien or mermaid. You will also see them invent unique fantasy beings and creatures from their own imagination based on all of the knowledge and experience they have amassed. For children who display more advanced role-play skills, they will move on from playing a generic role like 'a teacher' or 'farmer', to assuming the character of people that they know copying their familiar language, speech patterns, intonation and mannerisms.

We play to learn lots of things. We learn lots.

EVIE-LOU, AGE 4

DISPOSITION

CURIOSITY

PLAY FEEDS CURIOSITY
IN A SPACE THAT IS
OPEN ENDED, FLEXIBLE
AND CHANGEABLE

MESS

A GOOD PLAY-BASED ENVIRONMENT WILL ALWAYS HAVE A HEALTHY AMOUNT OF CHILD-GENERATED MESS ON ANY GIVEN DAY: THE ODD HANDPRINT ON THE WALL, SPLASH OF PAINT ON THE LINO AND SPRINKLE OF GLITTER IN THE DOORMAT!

I like to play with the animals because they are my favourite and when I play with them I feel happy.

JAMMY, AGE 4

PLAY IS THE ANSWER TO THE QUESTION, 'HOW DOES ANYTHING NEW COME ABOUT?'

– JEAN PIAGET

WHAT IS PLAY?

For all humans, children and adults, what we play is what we know and what we experience. Sometimes our play will replicate real life, sometimes fantasy and often a mixture of both. Children can imagine possibilities, think of possible outcomes to a specific scenario and then test their thoughts. Role play is one of the only places where children are actively able to mix the realms of fantasy and reality either as a solo experience or alongside others. It is the element of play that keeps them safe.

PRACTITIONER NOTE

Keep your 'CORE' play resourcing (simple) and (un-themed.)

Cardboard boxes, tubes, crates, fabric and den making materials.

Then enhance it with 'REAL' objects that you have collected to support a theme or interest.

CONSIDER THE SPACE IN YOUR EARLY YEARS SETTING ...

In his text *Can I Go and Play Now?*, Greg Bottrill discusses what children need from the adults in their play settings:

Is the space calming? Is it a home for the children? Or, does it represent your own idea of what you think an early years 'classroom' should look like? Is it decorated with online-acquired displays, posters and huge intricate boards in garish primary hues? We need to begin to ask ourselves: what is it that children need around them to truly learn, feel safe and feel like the classroom is somewhere that they can call their own?

Your objective should be to create a Universe where children can operate. One that is their Universe – not the adult's idea of what that Universe should look like.

PLAY FUELS YOUR CREATIVITY, TICKLES YOUR INNER CHILD AND NURTURES YOUR SOUL.

– CLAUDIA BLACK

MOVING SPACES

Successful play spaces offer movement and physical activity with space and features that allow a range of energetic and strength building play experiences.

OUTDOOR FUN

MOST CHILDREN FIND PLAYING OUTDOORS GREAT FUN — WHATEVER THE WEATHER. CHILDREN ARE NATURALLY HAPPY WHEN THEY ARE ABLE TO PHYSICALLY MOVE, PLAY AND CREATE. HAPPY LEARNERS MAKE SUCCESSFUL LEARNERS.

I just like playing with the bricks because I get to make a big massive house. I feel happy because someone gets to play with me with the bricks and that's what I like.

TRISTAIN, AGE 5

LORIS MALAGUZZI (1920–1994)

Malaguzzi studied teaching at university for the duration of the Second World War and became a schoolteacher in 1946. For context, Italy was left in a very bad way after Second World War and it is thought that up to 180,000 children were left on the streets of Rome alone after the country overthrew its fascist leaders.

One particular village became so upset with the government's lack of commitment to national development that they sold all of the village's horses and even a German tank to self-fund the materials for a school. The people of the village then spent a week building the school for all the local children that were left without any means to learn after the damage done during the Second World War.

It was when Malaguzzi visited this village he became inspired by the motivation to give the children somewhere to learn. This is where he founded the Reggio Emilia approach to education. The Reggio Emilia approach is notoriously difficult to define aside from the core principle that children have a born capacity to learn and develop and it is their right to do so.

This very humanist view of early years education has inspired curricula like Whāriki and has shaped much of the modern way of teaching children.

A GOOD SING

THERE IS LOTS OF JOY IN HAVING A GOOD SING. THERE IS ALSO A GREAT DEAL OF ACADEMIC RESEARCH THAT SAYS THAT SINGING HAS A SIGNIFICANT IMPACT ON CHILDREN'S PHONOLOGICAL AWARENESS.

CHILDREN WHO ENGAGE IN REGULAR SINGING AND MUSICAL ACTIVITIES MAKE SIGNIFICANTLY BETTER PROGRESS THAN THOSE WHO DON'T.

WE NEED TO SING MORE IN EARLY YEARS SETTINGS AND TO ENCOURAGE CHILDREN TO SING MORE IN THEIR PLAY. NOT ONLY BECAUSE OF THE IMPACT THAT IT CAN HAVE ON LEARNING AND DEVELOPMENT BUT BECAUSE OF ALL OF THE OTHER HUGE BENEFITS THAT CHILDREN GAIN FROM BEING EXPOSED TO IT.

SO, GO AND WARM UP YOUR VOCAL CHORDS...

ALISTAIR BRYCE-CLEGG

THE TRULY GREAT ADVANCES OF THIS GENERATION WILL BE MADE BY THOSE WHO CAN MAKE OUTRAGEOUS CONNECTIONS, AND ONLY A MIND WHICH KNOWS HOW TO PLAY CAN DO THAT.

– NAGLE JACKSON

CHILD LED PLANNING

- ✱ MOVE AWAY from the yearly topic planner
- ✱ BE LED by children's interests
- ✱ FIND OUT what they know
- ✱ ADD your own pinch (or large blob) of expertise
- ✱ Create a 'something' that pulls it all together
- ✱ Assess, Assess, Assess

PRIVATE SPEECH

The work of Vygotsky and Piaget tells us about 'Private Speech' in play. It is most evident in children from the age of two to seven. It is literally where children will talk to themselves during play. Although this talk is audible it is not directed at anyone else. It is like an internal dialogue where children coach themselves through an activity or situation.

A strong correlation has been found between children who use a high level of self-talk and the achievement of success in the task that they are engaged in.

NOT ALWAYS SMILES AND LAUGHTER

PLAY IS NOT ALWAYS ACCOMPANIED BY SMILES AND LAUGHTER. MENTAL TENSION MAY ARISE AS PLAYERS STRIVE TO PERFORM WELL; BUT, AS PLAY IS ALWAYS SELF-CHOSEN, SO IS ANY MENTAL TENSION THAT ACCOMPANIES IT. IF THE TENSION BECOMES TOO GREAT, REACHING THE LEVEL OF DISTRESS, THE PLAYER IS FREE TO QUIT OR CHANGE THE STRUCTURE OF THE PLAY AT ANY TIME AND THEREBY RELIEVE THE TENSION. IF AN ACTIVITY BECOMES COMPULSIVE, SO THAT THE PERSON CONTINUES AT IT DESPITE A HIGH DEGREE OF MENTAL DISTRESS, THEN WE ARE INCLINED TO SAY THAT THE ACTIVITY IS NO LONGER PLAY.

ALISTAIR BRYCE-CLEGG

THE CHILD AMIDST HIS BAUBLES IS LEARNING THE ACTION OF LIGHT, MOTION, GRAVITY, MUSCULAR FORCE....

— RALPH WALDO EMERSON

CHILDREN CANNOT BOUNCE OFF THE WALLS IF WE TAKE AWAY THE WALLS.

– ERIN KENNY

A FOUR LETTER WORD!

IN CERTAIN CIRCLES THESE DAYS 'PLAY' HAS BECOME A 'FOUR LETTER WORD'! THE PROBLEM IS THAT SOME PEOPLE DON'T MAKE THE CONNECTION BETWEEN PLAY AND LEARNING. WE NEED TO MAKE SURE THAT WE UNDERSTAND HOW THE ENVIRONMENT THAT WE CREATE NOT ONLY ALLOWS CHILDREN TO HAVE LOTS OF OPPORTUNITIES TO PLAY FREELY, BUT ALSO SUPPORTS THEIR LEARNING THROUGH CHALLENGE.

THE PLAY OF CHILDREN IS NOT RECREATION; IT MEANS EARNEST WORK. PLAY IS THE PUREST INTELLECTUAL PRODUCTION OF THE HUMAN BEING.

- FRIEDRICH FROEBEL

Pop goes the Weasel

Half a pound of tuppenny rice
Half a pound of treacle
That's the way the money goes
Pop goes the weasel

Up and down the city road
In and out of the Eagle
That's the way the money goes
Pop goes the weasel

Pop Goes the Weasel - Making use of Cockney rhyming slang, this children's nursery rhyme tells a precautionary tale to people who aren't careful with their money. In Cockney rhyming slang, to 'POP' something is to pawn it and a 'weasel' is a coat (Weasel and Stoat). The rhyme suggests that if you spend your money on rice and treacle (frivolous food) you will have to sacrifice something much more important later on to get by. In the second verse, 'the Eagle' is a pub that was popularised by Charles Dickens so further warns us about the dangers of going to the pub and spending your money on alcohol!

Cus it makes us laugh a lot.

REGGIE, AGE 4

ENJOY THE POWER, MAGIC
AND INDIVIDUALITY OF
CHILDREN'S IMAGINATIONS.
MAKE SURE THAT THEIR DAY
IS FILLED WITH OPPORTUNITIES
TO ABSORB THEMSELVES IN
THE PROCESS OF PLAY.

ALISTAIR
BRYCE-CLEGG

REFERENCES

January 6: Rubin, K. (2015) Children in Peer Groups in Rubin, *K. et al Handbook of Child Psychology Vol 3.* Wiley: New York.

January 8: For more on play therapy visit https://playtherapy.org.uk/

January 10: For more on the work of Stuart Brown MD visit https://www.playcore.com/drstuartbrown

January 11: Neaum, S. (2017) *What Comes Before Phonics?* SAGE Publications: London.

Goddard Blythe, S. (2011) Physical foundations for learning in House, R. *Too much too soon.* Stroud: Hawthorne Press.

January 20: Andrews, M. (2012) *Exploring Play for Early Childhood Studies.* SAGE Publications: London.

January 24: Gray, P. (2013) *Free to Learn: Why Unleashing the Instinct to Play Will Make Our Children Happier, More Self-Reliant, and Better Students for Life.* Basic Books: New York.

January 25: Spinka, M., Newberry, R.C. and Bekoff, M. (2001) Mammalian Play: Training for the Unexpected, *The Quarterly Review of Biology* 76:2: 141-168. https://doi.org/10.1086/393866

January 29: For more on the work of Heidi Kaduson visit https://www.heidigkaduson.com/

February 10: Isaacs, S. (1937) *The Educational Value of the Nursery School.* The Nursery School Association: UK.

February 13: For more on the work and life of Loris Malaguzzi visit https://www.reggiochildren.it/en/reggio-emilia-approach/loris-malaguzzi/

February 16: Bilton, H. (2014) *Playing Outside.* London: Routledge.

February 22: Gray, P. (2013) *Free to Learn: Why Unleashing the Instinct to Play Will Make Our Children Happier, More Self-Reliant, and Better Students for Life.* Basic Books: New York.

March 10: For more on the work of Vince Gowman visit https://www.vincegowmon.com/about-vince/

March 13: For more on The National Institute for Play visit http://www.nifplay.org/

March 16: For more on the work of Stuart Brown visit https://www.playcore.com/drstuartbrown

March 24: For more on the work of Kay Redfield Jamison visit https://www.hopkinsmedicine.org/profiles/results/directory/profile/5353763/kay-jamison

April 4: Gray, P. (2013) *Free to Learn: Why Unleashing the Instinct to Play Will Make Our Children Happier, More Self-Reliant, and Better Students for Life*. Basic Books: New York.

April 9: Dobson, F. (2004) *Getting Serious about Play*. London: Department of Culture, Media and Sport.

April 21: Isaacs, S. (1937) *The Educational Value of the Nursery School*. The Nursery School Association: Great Britain.

April 26: Bilton, H. (2014) *Playing Outside*. London: Routledge.

May 2: Kambouri-Danos, M. (2020) Early years and play in Jones, K. (Ed) *Challenging Gender Stereotypes in Education*. SAGE Publications: London.

May 11: For more on the work of Stuart Brown visit https://www.playcore.com/drstuartbrown

June 2: Thorpe, K. (2019) Resourcing the spirit of the child: Creativity in the contemporary classroom, in Ogier, S. (Ed) *Teaching and Broad and Balanced Curriculum in Primary Schools*. SAGE Publications: London.

June 8: Gray, P. (2013) *Free to Learn: Why Unleashing the Instinct to Play Will Make Our Children Happier, More Self-Reliant, and Better Students for Life*. Basic Books: New York.

June 25: Bottrill, G. (2018) *Can I Go and Play Now?* SAGE Publications: London.

July 9: Andrews, M. (2012) *Exploring Play for Early Childhood Studies*. SAGE Publications: London.

Moyles, J. (1994) *The Excellence of Play*. Buckingham: OUP.

July 12: Bilton, H. 2014, *Playing Outside*. London: Routledge.

July 19: For more on the work of Erika Christakis visit http://erikachristakis.com/author/bio/

August 18: Gray, P. (2013) *Free to Learn: Why Unleashing the Instinct to Play Will Make Our Children Happier, More Self-Reliant, and Better Students for Life*. Basic Books: New York.

September 10: Csikszentmihalyi, Mihaly, (1990) *Flow: The Psychology of Optimal Experience*. New York: Harper & Row.

September 23: Andrews, M. (2012) *Exploring Play for Early Childhood Studies*. SAGE Publications: London.

September 26: For more on the work of Stuart Brown visit https://www.playcore.com/drstuartbrown

September 30: Huizinga, J. (1955, originally published in 1938) *Homo Ludens: A Study of the Play Element in Culture*. Beacon Press, Boston.

October 8: Bottrill, G. (2018) *Can I Go and Play Now?* SAGE Publications: London.

October 27: McEvoy, J. and McMahon, S. (2018) *Child Centered Planning in the Early Years Foundation Stage*. SAGE Publications: London.

November 2: Clark, R. (2020) *Childhood in Society for the Early Years 3rd edition.* SAGE Publications: London.

November 5: For more on the work of Vince Gowman visit https://www.vincegowmon.com/about-vince/

November 6: Andrews, M. (2012) *Exploring Play for Early Childhood Studies.* SAGE Publications: London.

November 11: Gray, P. (2013) *Free to Learn: Why Unleashing the Instinct to Play Will Make Our Children Happier, More Self-Reliant, and Better Students for Life.* Basic Books: New York.

November 13: For more about Dr Stuart Brown visit https://www.playcore.com/drstuartbrown

November 18: Palaiologou, I. (2020) Child Observation: *A Guide for Students of Early Childhood 4th Edition.* SAGE Publications: London.

November 26: Bilton, H. (2014) *Playing Outside.* London: Routledge.

December 14: Bottrill, G. (2018) *Can I Go and Play Now?* SAGE Publications: London.

Lightning Source UK Ltd.
Milton Keynes UK
UKHW050726030520
362579UK00003B/92